Approaches to learning and teaching

Business & Economics

a toolkit for international teachers

Andrew Gillespie

Series Editors: Paul Ellis and Lauren Harris

CAMBRIDGE
UNIVERSITY PRESS

University Printing House, Cambridge CB2 8BS, United Kingdom

One Liberty Plaza, 20th Floor, New York, NY 10006, USA

477 Williamstown Road, Port Melbourne, VIC 3207, Australia

4843/24, 2nd Floor, Ansari Road, Daryaganj, Delhi – 110002, India

79 Anson Road, #06–04/06, Singapore 079906

Cambridge University Press is part of the University of Cambridge.

It furthers the University's mission by disseminating knowledge in the pursuit of education, learning and research at the highest international levels of excellence.

www.cambridge.org
Information on this title: www.cambridge.org/9781316645949 (Paperback)

First published 2017

20 19 18 17 16 15 14 13 12 11 10 9 8 7 6 5 4 3 2 1

Printed in Great Britain by CPI Group (UK) Ltd, Croydon CR0 4YY

A catalogue record for this publication is available from the British Library

ISBN 978-1-316-64594-9 Paperback

Contents

Acknowledgements

The authors and publishers acknowledge the following sources of copyright material and are grateful for the permissions granted.

Cover bgblue/Getty Images; Fig. 3.3a Erik Isakson/Getty Images; Fig 3.3b David Tise/Getty Images; Fig 3.3c Dave & Les Jacobs/ Getty Images; Fig 3.3d Zero Creatives/Getty Images; Fig 4.1a Monty Rakusen/Getty Images; Fig 4.1b Caiaimage/Robert Daly/Getty Images; Fig 4.1c gruizza/Getty Images; Fig 4.1d Ariel Skelley/Getty Images; Fig 6.1a HeliRY/Getty Images; Fig 6.2b LIVINUS/Getty Images; Fig 6.1c kevinjeon00/Getty Images; Fig 6.1d Julian Love/ Getty Images; Fig 6.2a Lester Lefkowitz/Getty Images; Fig 6.2b Anatolii Babii/Getty Images; Fig 6.2c kevinjeon00/Getty Images; Fig 6.2d Latitude Stock/Getty Images; Fig 7.4 Caiaimage/ Sam Edwards/ Getty Images; Fig 8.3 Ariel Skelley/Getty Images; Fig 9.1 Dav & Lee Jacobs/Getty Images; Fig 10.2 Hero Images/Getty Images; Fig 11.1 Sam Edwards/Getty Images; Fig 11.2 Klaus Vedfelt/ Getty Images; Fig 11.3 Paula French/EyeEm/Getty Images; Fig 12.1 mf-guddyx/Getty Images; Fig 12.2 John Lamb/Getty Images; Fig 12.4 asiseeit/Getty Images; Fig 12.5 Heritage Images/Getty Images

1

Introduction to the series by the editors

1 Approaches to learning and teaching Business & Economics

This series of books is the result of close collaboration between Cambridge University Press and Cambridge International Examinations, both departments of the University of Cambridge. The books are intended as a companion guide for teachers, to supplement your learning and provide you with extra resources for the lessons you are planning. Their focus is deliberately not syllabus-specific, although occasional reference has been made to programmes and qualifications. We want to invite you to set aside for a while assessment objectives and grading, and take the opportunity instead to look in more depth at how you teach your subject and how you motivate and engage with your students.

The themes presented in these books are informed by evidence-based research into what works to improve students' learning and pedagogical best practices. To ensure that these books are first and foremost practical resources, we have chosen not to include too many academic references, but we have provided some suggestions for further reading.

We have further enhanced the books by asking the authors to create accompanying lesson ideas. These are described in the text and can be found in a dedicated space online. We hope the books will become a dynamic and valid representation of what is happening now in learning and teaching in the context in which you work.

Our organisations also offer a wide range of professional development opportunities for teachers. These range from syllabus- and topic-specific workshops and large-scale conferences to suites of accredited qualifications for teachers and school leaders. Our aim is to provide you with valuable support, to build communities and networks, and to help you both enrich your own teaching methodology and evaluate its impact on your students.

Each of the books in this series follows a similar structure. In the first chapter, we have asked our authors to consider the essential elements of their subject, the main concepts that might be covered in a school curriculum, and why these are important. The next chapter gives you a brief guide on how to interpret a syllabus or subject guide, and how to plan a programme of study. The authors will encourage you to think too about what is not contained in a syllabus and how you can pass on your own passion for the subject you teach.

The main body of the text takes you through those aspects of learning and teaching which are widely recognised as important. We would like to stress that there is no single recipe for excellent teaching, and that different schools, operating in different countries and cultures, will have strong traditions that should be respected. There is a growing consensus, however, about some important practices and approaches that need to be adopted if students are going to fulfil their potential and be prepared for modern life.

In the common introduction to each of these chapters we look at what the research says and the benefits and challenges of particular approaches. Each author then focuses on how to translate theory into practice in the context of their subject, offering practical lesson ideas and teacher tips. These chapters are not mutually exclusive but can be read independently of each other and in whichever order suits you best. They form a coherent whole but are presented in such a way that you can dip into the book when and where it is most convenient for you to do so.

The final two chapters are common to all the books in this series and are not written by the subject authors. Schools and educational organisations are increasingly interested in the impact that classroom practice has on student outcomes. We have therefore included an exploration of this topic and some practical advice on how to evaluate the success of the learning opportunities you are providing for your students. The book then closes with some guidance on how to reflect on your teaching and some avenues you might explore to develop your own professional learning.

We hope you find these books accessible and useful. We have tried to make them conversational in tone so you feel we are sharing good practice rather than directing it. Above all, we hope that the books will inspire you and enable you to think in more depth about how you teach and how your students learn.

Paul Ellis and Lauren Harris

Series Editors

2 Purpose and context

International research into educational effectiveness tells us that student achievement is influenced most by what teachers do in classrooms. In a world of rankings and league tables we tend to notice performance, not preparation, yet the product of education is more than just examinations and certification. Education is also about the formation of effective learning habits that are crucial for success within and beyond the taught curriculum.

The purpose of this series of books is to inspire you as a teacher to reflect on your practice, try new approaches and better understand how to help your students learn. We aim to help you develop your teaching so that your students are prepared for the next level of their education as well as life in the modern world.

This book will encourage you to examine the processes of learning and teaching, not just the outcomes. We will explore a variety of teaching strategies to enable you to select which is most appropriate for your students and the context in which you teach. When you are making your choice, involve your students: all the ideas presented in this book will work best if you engage your students, listen to what they have to say, and consistently evaluate their needs.

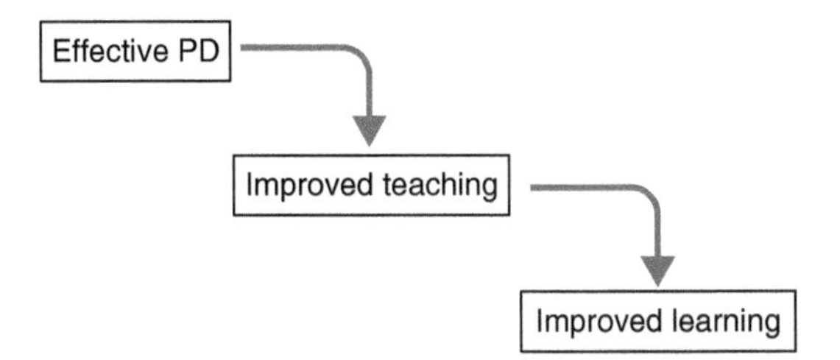

Cognitive psychologists, coaches and sports writers have noted how the aggregation of small changes can lead to success at the highest level. As teachers, we can help our students make marginal gains by guiding them in their learning, encouraging them to think and talk about how they are learning, and giving them the tools to monitor their success. If you take care of the learning, the performance will take care of itself.

When approaching an activity for the first time, or revisiting an area of learning, ask yourself if your students know how to:

- approach a new task and plan which strategies they will use
- monitor their progress and adapt their approach if necessary
- look back and reflect on how well they did and what they might do differently next time.

2 Approaches to learning and teaching Business & Economics

Effective learners understand that learning is an active process. We need to challenge and stretch our students and enable them to interrogate, analyse and evaluate what they see and hear. Consider whether your students:

- challenge assumptions and ask questions
- try new ideas and take intellectual risks
- devise strategies to overcome any barriers to their learning that they encounter.

As we discuss in the chapters on **Active learning** and **Metacognition**, it is our role as teachers to encourage these practices with our students so that they become established routines. We can help students review their own progress as well as getting a snapshot ourselves of how far they are progressing by using some of the methods we explore in the chapter on **Assessment for Learning**.

Students often view the subject lessons they are attending as separate from each other, but they can gain a great deal if we encourage them to take a more holistic appreciation of what they are learning. This requires not only understanding how various concepts in a subject fit together, but also how to make connections between different areas of knowledge and how to transfer skills from one discipline to another. As our students successfully integrate disciplinary knowledge, they are better able to solve complex problems, generate new ideas and interpret the world around them.

In order for students to construct an understanding of the world and their significance in it, we need to lead students into thinking habitually about why a topic is important on a personal, local and global scale. Do they realise the implications of what they are learning and what they do with their knowledge and skills, not only for themselves but also for their neighbours and the wider world? To what extent can they recognise and express their own perspective as well as the perspectives of others? We will consider how to foster local and global awareness, as well as personal and social responsibility, in the chapter on **Global thinking**.

As part of the learning process, some students will discover barriers to their learning: we need to recognise these and help students to overcome them. Even students who regularly meet success face their own challenges. We have all experienced barriers to our own learning at some point in our lives and should be able as teachers to empathise and share our own methods for dealing with these. In the chapter on **Inclusive education** we discuss how to make learning accessible for everyone and how to ensure that all students receive the instruction and support they need to succeed as learners.

Some students are learning through the medium of English when it is not their first language, while others may struggle to understand subject jargon even if they might otherwise appear fluent. For all students, whether they are learning through their first language or an additional language, language is a vehicle for learning. It is through language that students access the content of the lesson and communicate their ideas. So, as teachers, it is our responsibility to make sure that language isn't a barrier to learning. In the chapter on **Language awareness** we look at how teachers can pay closer attention to language to ensure that all students can access the content of a lesson.

Alongside a greater understanding of what works in education and why, we as teachers can also seek to improve how we teach and expand the tools we have at our disposal. For this reason, we have included a chapter in this book on **Teaching with digital technologies**, discussing what this means for our classrooms and for us as teachers. Institutes of higher education and employers want to work with students who are effective communicators and who are information literate. Technology brings both advantages and challenges and we invite you to reflect on how to use it appropriately.

This book has been written to help you think harder about the impact of your teaching on your students' learning. It is up to you to set an example for your students and to provide them with opportunities to celebrate success, learn from failure and, ultimately, to succeed.

We hope you will share what you gain from this book with other teachers and that you will be inspired by the ideas that are presented here. We hope that you will encourage your school leaders to foster a positive environment that allows both you and your students to meet with success and to learn from mistakes when success is not immediate. We hope too that this book can help in the creation and continuation of a culture where learning and teaching are valued and through which we can discover together what works best for each and every one of our students.

3 The nature of the subject

Introduction

In this chapter we discuss the nature of Business and Economics and consider some of the joys and demands of teaching and learning these subjects.

The nature of Business and Economics

Economics is a tremendous subject to help students understand so many of the things that they see in the news such as inflation, trade deficits, share price movements and unemployment. Economics helps students to develop valuable analytical skills and learn to use theory to unpick an issue. For example: Why is the economy growing slowly, and how does it affect different groups such as employees and firms? Economics considers how the government might influence the economy and the actions governments can take in terms of specific markets and the economy as a whole.

Economists build models to explain how the different parts of the economy work and how they fit together (see Figure 3.1). A low interest rate, for example, makes it cheaper to borrow, which increases spending, which increases demand, which increases output, which reduces unemployment and creates economic growth. This is an analytical chain. Students then consider why the model or theory may not work – what are the limitations of this model? What are the assumptions behind it? What would happen if they changed some of these assumptions?

Economics appeals to the logical mind: students who like puzzles and who want to follow an argument through its different stages love this subject. Students can look at the world around them and analyse it; they can explain why house prices in their area are relatively high or low and they can assess whether current government policies are likely to be an effective way of reducing a budget deficit.

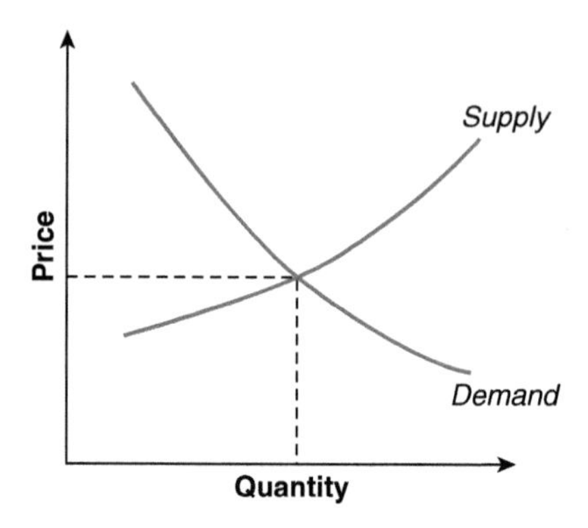

Figure 3.1: Economists use the supply and demand model to explain changes in many different markets. This model can help explain wages, prices of products, currency movement, changes in share prices and rents.

Students who do well in Economics often enjoy Maths and Physics although its appeal is far broader than this. It is a subject that is much valued by universities and employers, and keeps many doors open, whether or not a student wants to go on to study it later in life.

Business also allows students to connect with the world around them. It involves analysing decisions in a range of areas such as whether to target a new group of customers, how best to raise finance, how to reward staff and how to become more efficient. Studying Business provides an insight into many fascinating areas such as marketing, finance, human resources and operations (see Figure 3.2). These are issues that students encounter every day, for example: Why do I prefer one brand to another? Why have the profits of a company fallen? Why are redundancies being made at a local business?

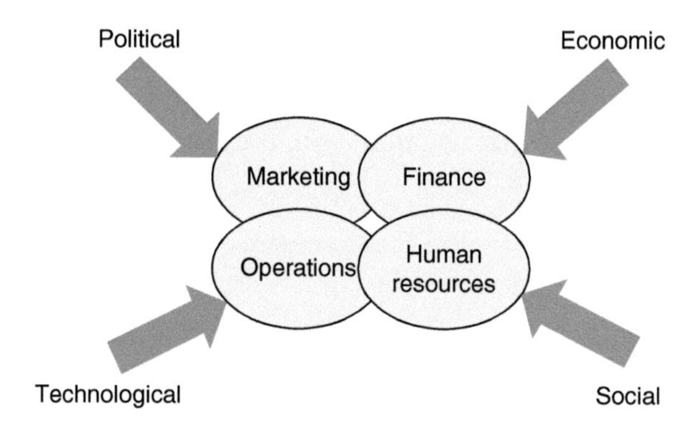

Figure 3.2: Business Studies involves an analysis of the internal functions of an organisation and the relationship between these and the outside world.

Teacher Tip

If you are trying to make a comparison between Economics and Business, use an example of a change in something like interest rates. Why the interest rate has changed and the effect of this on consumers, firms and the government is Economics. How a particular business might respond to this change or be affected by it is Business.

By studying Business, students learn the importance of context – the right decision depends on the situation. There are no simple answers – you need to find out about objectives, different stakeholder perspectives and the particular business situation. Students develop the ability to consider alternatives, to analyse issues from a range of perspectives and decide between options. They develop the skills needed to assess a situation, to weigh up arguments and to make judgements. Studying Business develops valuable critical thinking and decision-making skills, which are useful in many fields and are an important part of students' development as independent thinkers.

LESSON IDEA ONLINE 3.1: EVALUATION EXERCISE

Use this lesson idea to develop activities that encourage students to evaluate and support their judgements.

What differences are there between studying Economics and studying Business?

Studying Economics provides a level of certainty for students. They can identify a problem, select the appropriate economic theory and apply it. They have a set of tools to analyse and evaluate questions. If they have learnt and understood the models, they can feel fairly confident about how well they have analysed an issue.

Business has less certainty. For example, students may have learnt the marketing mix but the question is actually about applying the marketing mix to a given type of product. This context-based approach suits students who can think flexibly and like to debate. There is rarely a single correct answer in Business.

The level of Maths required by students is also worth considering. Many believe that Economics is more mathematically demanding than Business. While this is certainly true at degree level, I am less sure about the levels below this. Economics requires many mathematical skills such as the ability to produce and interpret diagrams and charts, and to undertake a variety of calculations. However, Business students also need to be comfortable undertaking calculations and interpreting a wide range of data to support their arguments. There are fewer diagrams and models but Business students have to appreciate the significance of many business indicators (such as market share, profitability, efficiency, productivity). Students also have to understand the links between data to consider how this might influence decision-making. This means that the numerical demands of Business should not be underestimated.

What do I need to teach the two subjects?

Teaching Economics involves a new language (with terms such as 'marginal costs', 'allocative efficiency' and 'GDP') and new concepts. As a teacher, you have a clear body of knowledge and theory to cover and a fairly clear structure in terms of what to teach and in what order. The challenge is to help students to apply the theory, manipulate models and diagrams, and be confident enough to explain unfamiliar data and policies.

In Business, the language and concepts are more accessible. Most people could sit in a Business lesson and understand much of what was being said without having studied it. However, Business remains demanding because the development of students' arguments needs to be fully contextualised (see Figure 3.3) – there is little 'pure' theory they can roll out because it all depends on what is happening in the given business. Students cannot simply learn, say, the benefits of buying a franchise because the actual benefits that are relevant depend on who is buying it, why they are buying it, what the franchise is and the specific terms and conditions. Teaching Business needs to be case study-based – it is about appreciating how the meaning of productivity varies from a hotel to a car manufacturer, or how the importance of TV advertising varies for different companies, from a major chocolate bar producer to a local florist. You need activities that encourage debate and develop different perspectives; you need a good portfolio of scenarios and 'what if' questions.

Figure 3.3: In Business the context is extremely important. For example, the ways you reward a waiter, a doctor, a lawyer and a cleaner are likely to be very different.

Teacher Tip

Business news websites can be good for finding relevant case studies.

In Economics, the challenge is to help students understand how to use the theory; for example, they need plenty of practice manipulating the diagrams effectively. There are many opportunities for activities in lessons where you can easily assess students' learning. You could ask students to show what happens in a market if demand increases or what happens to aggregate demand when income tax is reduced. For these types of tasks, students could be asked to produce their answers on mini whiteboards and show their responses, allowing you to assess their understanding.

Business does have some similar topics – for example, break-even is ideal for 'what if' type activities. However, a great deal of Business is about discussion – there is no clear-cut answer so you need to encourage students to think through what might affect a particular issue and to make a judgement. There is less opportunity to say 'that is right' (or wrong), so feedback is more about the quality of an argument or judgement. When you first start teaching Business, it often feels slightly less structured than Economics – you have fewer frameworks to use with students and fewer right/wrong assessments. The positive side is that it gives justification for discussion that can provide truly engaging lessons and at the end of it you have helped your students to become very flexible thinkers.

Teacher Tip

Use the questioning technique of 'what if ...?' to keep students' thinking flexible.

One idea is to ask students to write an answer to a question about a car manufacturer and then think 'what if' it was about a search engine business such as Google or Baidu? Or a state-owned business? Or a business with limited funds?

Teaching Business and Economics

Both Business and Economics are constantly changing subjects. The business winners and losers from last year can be very different this year;

the star economies of the previous decade can suddenly falter. To keep our subjects relevant, we need to constantly review and update our resources. The case study of Kodak failing to move into digital cameras probably seems increasingly less relevant to students who may struggle to understand what 35mm film is. We need to scour the news regularly to see how we can build a lesson based on current events. Even if it is just a starter or plenary, bringing in some recent data or issue can help students to appreciate that this is helping them understand the world around them.

LESSON IDEA 3.2: START A BLOG/NEWS DIARY

Encourage your students to start a blog or news diary to help them find out what is happening in business and the economy around them. Alternatively, ask them all to bring in a news story related to the topic you have been studying.

Both subjects should be lively, relevant and engaging. Students should be able to relate their studies to the world around them and it should be possible to provoke exciting debates and discussions. Use the news and bring in business and economic issues as they happen – that's when students can really see these subjects come to life.

Summary

The key points to remember in this chapter are:

- As teachers of Business and/or Economics we are fortunate to be teaching subjects that can interest, enthuse and inspire students.
- Both subjects develop students' abilities to analyse and make judgements that build logically on the arguments made. These skills will be valuable whatever students go on to do.
- There are important differences in the challenges that teaching each subject provides.

4 Key considerations

Introduction

In this chapter, we look at some of the key considerations when teaching Business and Economics from the perspective of the teacher and the students.

What have I learnt from teaching Business and Economics?

Among the many things I have learnt in 20 years of teaching these subjects are:

- **Don't just talk at students.** However fascinating you may be, students cannot concentrate for too long and they probably won't remember much of what you said! It will be a much more productive lesson if students are involved and help shape it. Get them working on an analysis of a case study, analysing economic data or presenting on government policy.
- **Plan the journey, not just the outcome.** Think about what you want students to achieve by the end of the lesson and how they can get there for themselves. Have you built in activities for shared working? Have they had the chance to discuss and review before recommending a business strategy? Remember, you don't have to do it all – let students do more of the work.
- **Plan but don't over-plan.** Have a structure to your lesson but be careful of planning every single minute. Keep enough flexibility to respond to things that emerge in discussions and activities. Something you cover may link to a business or economics item in the news that you want to refer to, for example.
- **Check that students are learning.** Regularly check what is understood and which areas are unclear so that time is used in a productive and focused way.
- **It should be fun.** There is nothing that says learning has to be overly serious. If you get a group of students engaged with the

subject, there is a buzz in the class and often plenty of laughter because they are enjoying working together on something that engages them.

- **Don't underestimate students.** Don't assume they are not interested, don't assume they cannot do it and don't aim low with tasks setting. Aim high–they will appreciate this and go with you.

Challenges

Using numbers

Numeracy is an important part of both Business and Economics. For some students, it is an aspect of the subject they can struggle with. Some lack strong mathematical skills, some simply lack confidence; whatever the reasons for this, it can lead them to avoid the numbers side of these subjects. However, an understanding of the significance of data is essential to these subjects. You can only really understand the context of a business situation if you can analyse factors such as its financial situation, the market and the external environment. You can only really assess an economic policy if you analyse some of the consequences numerically. We therefore have to build students' skills and confidence when dealing with data.

Teacher Tip

- Keep the numbers simple at first. For example, don't show students an actual balance sheet and don't ask them to analyse a price elasticity of -1.856 because these scenarios are too complex. Use basic figures to make it simpler to follow. It is easier to calculate the percentage change in price from £10 to £11, for example, than from £4.55 to £4.62. Get the foundations sorted before building higher.
- When setting a task based around numbers, see whether making the outcome particularly large or small, or making the change particularly noticeable, helps with the analysis. Commenting on a change in profitability from 5% to 4.8% may be difficult but a fall from 5% to 0.5% is immediately more thought-provoking.

LESSON IDEA ONLINE 4.1: HELPING STUDENTS TO USE DATA

Use this lesson idea to highlight the value of calculations and interpreting data by providing a context and having questions in which numbers support the analysis.

Here are some things to think about when teaching numeracy:

- **Be clear** what it is you are trying to show and try to reach a point where students can explain the underlying theory without numbers. Explain what you are going to calculate and why the concept matters – ask 'What are we using the numbers for?'
- **Be structured. Explain the method used, carefully and precisely.** For example:
  a total revenue = price × quantity sold = $10 × 5000 = $50,000
  b total variable costs = variable cost per unit × number of units sold = $4 × 5000 = $20,000
  c total costs = total variable costs + fixed costs = $20,000 + $10,000 = $30,000
  d profit = total revenue – total costs = $50,000 – $30,000.

Teacher Tip

Keep the same structure when doing calculations. Avoid:

- changing your terminology (e.g. switching from 'turnover' to 'sales' to 'revenue')
- jumping stages (e.g. if you just jump to Total Costs = $20,000 + $10,000 without showing where the total variable costs came from, this will confuse some students)
- letting those who can do it easily dominate the feedback.

Think around the numerical topics. Examiners could look at mathematical topics from a number of different angles so be prepared for the unexpected. For example, perhaps you and your students are used to calculating market growth over time. Your typical question might be: If sales rise from $40,000 to $50,000, how much has the market grown? Answer: 25%. But what if the question was: Sales have grown 25% and are now $50,000. What were sales originally? Or, if sales are $40,000 and grow by 25%, what would they be now? There are clearly three elements to this topic: original sales, new sales and the market growth rate. Prepare students for any of the possible questions that might be asked around this.

- **Be reassuring.** An understanding of a mathematical concept will gain some marks even if a student struggles to carry out the calculation completely accurately. Even if they make a mathematical error, any judgements they make based on their answer will be credited using the Own Figure Rule, which means they get credit for the method and underlying understanding as well as the actual answer.

Learning to apply

One of the challenges for Business students is learning how to apply what they know to a range of business contexts (see Figure 4.1). The marketing activities to promote sports cars are very different from the marketing activities linked to fruit juices. It is no good simply learning lists of points – the knowledge has to be put into action. Help your students by creating different scenarios that you keep relating to. For example, consider different topics such as marketing, operations management and finance in contexts such as a school, a car manufacturer and a supermarket. However, it is not just about the type of business but also the situation that the business is in.

For example, what will vary if the business is:

- A growing business compared to one that has remained small?
- A multinational compared to a start-up?
- A non-profit organisation compared to a company owned by investors?

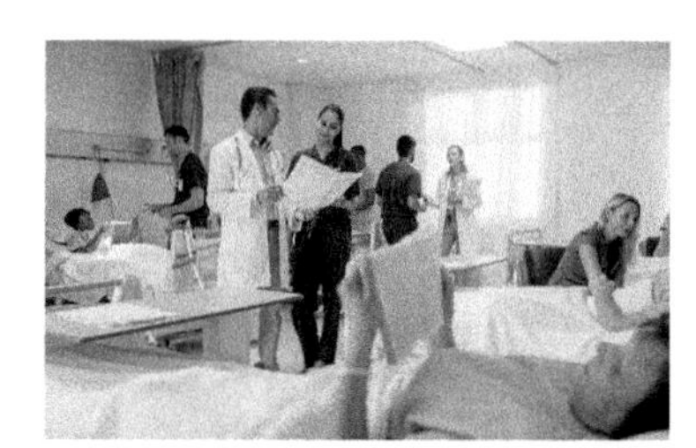

Figure 4.1: It is important to highlight the importance of the context when teaching Business and Economics. For example, the human resources and operations challenges in the different business contexts above are very different.

In Economics, you must also make sure that students can apply their understanding effectively. This means examining different economies and different markets. How might the price elasticity of supply vary in the short run to the long run? What about in agricultural markets compared to manufacturing?

Teacher Tip

You should regularly ask students to apply their understanding to different and unfamiliar situations. Once you have taught a topic such as the cause of inflation, provide a different situation to analyse, such as deflation, and see whether they can use the tools they have learnt to explain this.

Building evaluative skills

An important skill in Business and Economics is the ability to evaluate. The word itself can be a problem as it is not always clear to students what it means. It may be better to talk about 'judgement'. Students need to be able to weigh up, prioritise and make judgements.

Ways to develop this skill include:

- **Making the questions you set evaluative**
  'Explain how the government can reduce unemployment' tests understanding. 'To what extent is cutting unemployment benefits the best way for a government to reduce unemployment? will almost automatically generate judgement.

- **Developing an evaluative language**
  Is one option a 'priority'? What is the 'most significant' factor? What is the 'most important' issue? Is this action 'right'? When you set questions, ask questions and feed back on ideas, make sure that you are using and encouraging this language.

- **Challenging students constantly to think about what matters most**
  If you set a question asking for three factors, can you get students to put these in order and justify their choices? If there is a case for and against, which wins? Why?

Literacy

Problems with literacy can be a major barrier to success and many students need support in this area. In Economics, there is often substantial stimulus material with quite complex and technical language to read and understand under limited time conditions. Similarly in Business, there is often a case study that needs to be read very carefully and understood fully before attempting the questions. Understanding the context of a business is often key to producing good arguments and judgements. Being able to read extended passages of text and pull out the key points is very important in both subjects.

To develop students' literacy skills, we need to encourage them to read business and economics news stories.

Teacher Tip

Ways of improving literacy include asking students to:

- contribute to a regular blog
- produce a weekly news report
- keep their own diary of stories and events
- read economics and business articles in newspapers and magazines.

The danger is that students see such activities as tangential to their mainstream studies and their exams, and therefore do not spend much time on them. Sometimes they want to focus on the textbook and little else. So it is important to raise the status of these types of assignments – include reference to them in your reports, comment on them, assign them a grade or mark, make the contribution visible and refer to the work in lessons.

What challenges do students face?

The challenges of Business and Economics include:

- **Developing sustained arguments.** Your questioning and your feedback are key here to help students develop their arguments.
- **Answering the question.** Students often answer a version of the question they wished had been asked or provide an answer that outlines the arguments but does not actually directly address the question asked (see Figures 4.2 and 4.3).
- **Being flexible to respond to the context.** Most of us like to 'know things' and it comes as a bit of shock when we have to realise that this understanding is not fixed – what might be right can vary. For some students, this challenges the way that they have been thinking up until now. They need guidance and reassurance that in Business, for example, there is rarely a right answer – it depends on the context.

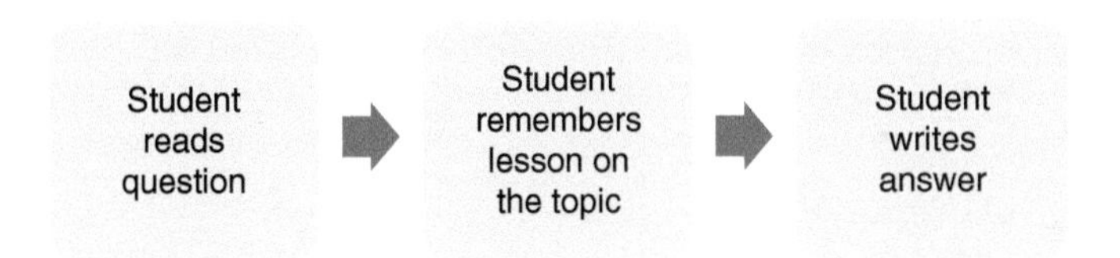

Figure 4.2: What tends to happen when students answer a question.

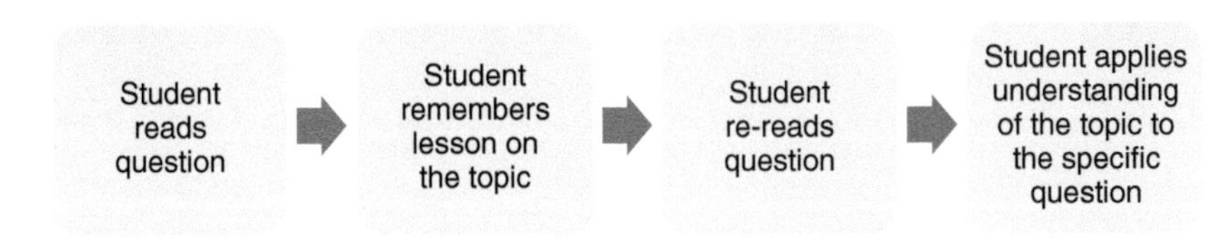

Figure 4.3: What we would like to happen when students answer a question.

Summary

The key points to remember in this chapter are:

- The specific challenges in Business and Economics include numeracy, learning how to apply ideas, literacy and evaluative skills. A number of ways of helping students in these areas have been considered.
- It is important for students to relate their learning to the real world in Business and Economics as this will engage them and help bring the topics to life. It also gives the theory a context, making it more meaningful.

Interpreting a syllabus

5

Introduction

This chapter shows you how to find your way around a syllabus and use it more effectively to support your teaching and your students' learning. The syllabus highlights the content we must cover in Business and Economics but these are ever-changing subjects with new issues emerging all the time – such as the UK's relationship with the European Union – so we should be willing to explore areas beyond the syllabus as well.

The syllabus

A syllabus sets out the topics that will be covered by the assessment. You should be able to cross-refer and identify where particular questions in the exams fit in relation to the syllabus. All areas of the syllabus should be assessed over a series of examinations; however, it is likely that some areas will be covered more than others. An understanding of supply and demand, for example, is fundamental to many Economics questions.

Highlight in your scheme of work which sections of the syllabus are being covered in any period of your course and make sure that you cover all the sections at some point. Use the same language and terminology in your teaching as are used in the syllabus. Look at all the syllabus content – any part of it can be drawn on for an examination.

Subject overview and subject content

The syllabus includes a subject overview. Give a copy of this to students to show them the 'big picture'. For example, students may find it useful to know before they start studying macroeconomics that they will consider how aggregate demand and aggregate supply interact, and they will consider how government policy can influence these. Remember that you do not have to teach the subject in the order set out in the syllabus.

Teacher Tip

The 'right' way to teach a subject will vary from teacher to teacher. For example, some people prefer to teach Business by focusing on the external environment first and then considering the impact on businesses and how businesses may react. Others prefer to examine what happens inside a business first. Some believe that you need to understand the strategy to be able to look at the tactical implications. Some believe that you need to understand the detail of the business before you can examine the broad strokes of strategy.

The key is whether there is a coherent narrative – if it flows easily, you have probably got the right order!

The key concepts

The syllabus may explain the underlying key concepts in the subject. For example, in one Business syllabus, it states that there are six concepts that underpin the subject as a whole. These are:

1 change
2 management
3 customer focus
4 innovation
5 creating value
6 strategy.

These concepts provide a useful reference point when covering any of the topics. For example, when studying operations you might consider:

1 What might lead us to **change** our operations activities?
2 What does **managing** operations involve?
3 How are operations decisions influenced by a **customer focus**?

4 What would an example of **innovation** in operations be?
5 How do operational activities **create value**?
6 What are examples of **strategic** operational decisions?

This focus on the concepts helps you to ensure that what you are teaching is aligned to the approach likely to be adopted in an exam.

Teacher Tip

You could take the key concepts and apply them to each of the subject sections. You may refer to these concepts in your schemes of work (see Figure 5.1).

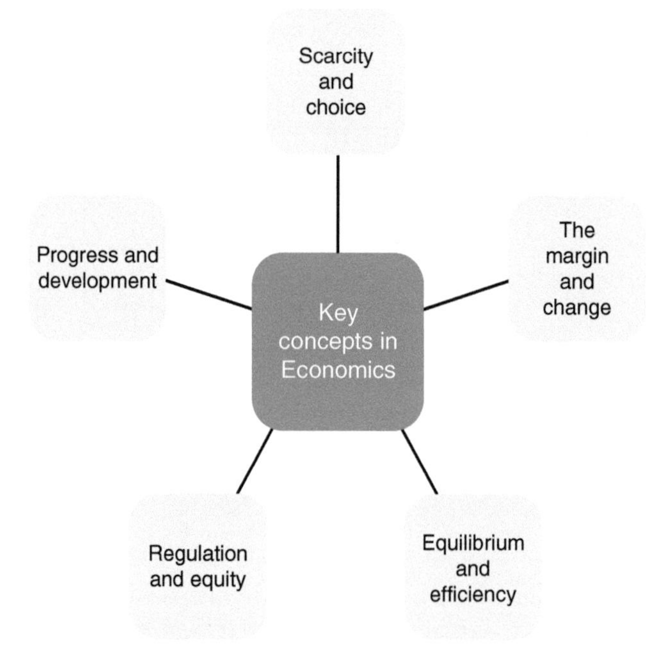

Figure 5.1: The key concepts in Economics.

LESSON IDEA ONLINE 5.1: APPLYING THE KEY CONCEPTS

This lesson idea can be used to help students understand how the key concepts relate to different aspects of the syllabus.

Assessment

Students need to know what examiners will assess, how they may assess it and what is rewarded.

The essentials of assessment include:

- how many papers there are
- what choices students have on different papers (sometimes students answer all the questions on a paper where they are supposed to choose, say, one from three)
- how long each paper lasts (this is essential to practise timings and make sure that the different parts of the paper have the right amount of time allocated to them)
- what content is assessed on each paper.

Assessment Objectives (AOs)

Be very clear what the assessment objectives are and how they are assessed by different command words. For example, evaluation is a higher-level skill than explanation; analysis is a higher-level skill than simply describing an issue. Students need to match command words such as 'state', 'examine' and 'discuss' to the appropriate assessment objectives.

Teacher Tip

It is vital that students understand the meaning of the assessment objectives so they know which skills to demonstrate. Make sure that students can explain the assessment objectives in their own words.

Subject aims

The syllabus includes a statement of the aims of the subject. This will help you to put the subject content into context and understand how it might be used and assessed.

For example, in one Business syllabus the subject aims provide teachers with valuable insights into how to approach topics:

- **Be aware of the scope of business including business locally and internationally.** That is a reminder to compare and contrast issues in the context of different organisations.
- **Adopt a critical understanding.** You should develop a questioning approach to every topic. Is creating a company better than being a sole trader? Why? Encourage students to question. Look at things from a different angle. For example, lower interest rates are likely to lead to more investment in an economy … but it does not always work like this – why not? Challenge students' understanding. Get them used to questioning a chain of argument. Is it always true? What makes it more or less likely to be true?
- **Consider a range of stakeholder perspectives.** How might a decision to move production to a lower-cost location overseas affect investors? Existing employees? Customers? Whether any decision is 'successful' or 'right' will depend on whose perspective is being considered.
- **Develop an awareness of political, economic, social, technological, legal, environmental and ethical issues associated with business activity.** Teaching must relate to the world around us. As a teacher, you must engage with the external environment and consider how that is affecting businesses; how businesses respond to such change and prepare for it.
- **Develop quantitative, problem-solving, decision-making and communication skills.** Students need to be familiar with numbers – they should be comfortable interpreting financial or marketing data, for example, and understanding the significance of it when making decisions and recommendations. This should influence the homework you set and the type of tasks you set in class.

Other useful information

Other useful information in the syllabus includes:

- the total guided hours (this gives you a guideline when putting together your scheme of work and homework)

- grade descriptors to give you an insight into what students need to do to achieve a top grade
- a glossary of the command words.

The syllabus and students

As exams approach, students should be highlighting all the words on the syllabus as they revise them to make sure that nothing has been missed. It is disappointing when students cannot access a question simply because they do not recognise a term such as 'allocative efficiency'. Students' understanding should be precise. This will require working through the syllabus word by word.

LESSON IDEA 5.2: RATING UNDERSTANDING

At the end of each syllabus section, ask students to rate their individual understanding using the RAG system: Red – not confident; Amber – some uncertainty; Green – confident (see Table 5.1). This will help you identify where you need to focus with each student.

Students submit this assessment to you and then, looking at their relative strengths and areas of uncertainty, you can match students for short discussions of topics. For example, pair up a student who is green in fiscal policy with someone who is red. The red student should ask the green student to explain the areas where they are struggling. If you find you have too many greens, give them extension questions to work on. If you have lots of reds on a topic, you may need to lead the discussion on this area.

Cover two or three different areas in the lesson to keep it moving, and to end up with a wide range of 'green' students as you find people who are confident in different areas.

TOPIC	RED: I need to do more on this	AMBER: I am generally comfortable with this topic	GREEN: I am very comfortable with this topic	Notes
Supply				
Demand			✔	No need to revise further
Elasticity of demand and supply	✔			Need to practise price changes given the price elasticity and impact on revenue
Movements vs shifts		✔		Ask teacher for a few more exercises but generally fine
How the market mechanism works	✔			Need to look at explaining how the market gets back to equilibrium when demand or supply shifts

Table 5.1: Students should be encouraged to identify the stages of their own learning and what they need to focus on.

What else do I need?

To gain a full picture of the subject and how to deliver it, you need some key documents (see Figure 5.2):

- **Past papers.** These will show how the content is assessed in practice, the style of question and the command words.
- **The mark schemes.** These show the typical content that might be expected in a student response and how examiners differentiate between a limited, reasonable and good response.
- **Principal Examiners' reports.** These show the issues that arose in a particular exam and what distinguished the stronger responses from the less successful ones. These reports are invaluable in terms of developing our teaching.

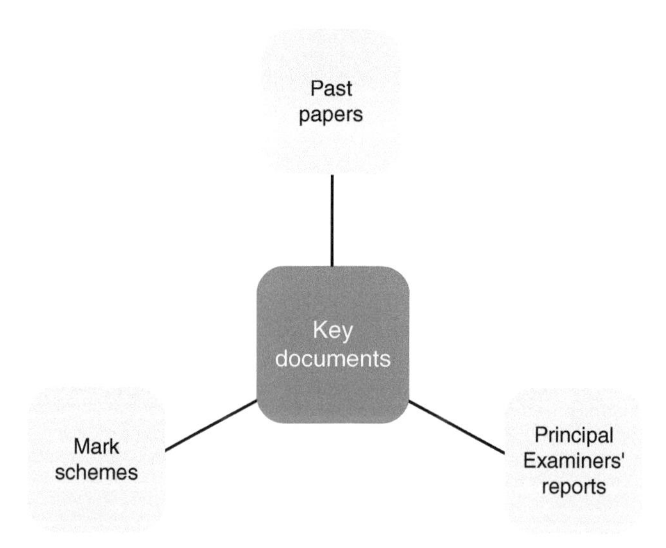

Figure 5.2: Key documents you need.

Teacher Tip

Your students may find it useful to read extracts of Principal Examiners' reports and write out in their own words the key points they found in them. They can compare their findings and discuss them. Why did one student think one issue was noteworthy whereas another did not? Sharing ideas is part of the learning process.

Summary

The key points to remember in this chapter are:

- The syllabus is your main point of reference for course content. Make sure that you have taught everything in the syllabus and used the same terminology in your teaching that is used in the syllabus itself. However, do explore areas beyond the syllabus if there is time.
- The syllabus will provide invaluable information on issues such as total guided learning hours and grade descriptors.
- Make sure your students are clear on the forms of assessment and the assessment objectives of each paper.
- Make use of past papers and examination reports, both of which will help bring the syllabus to life.

6 Active learning

What is active learning?

Active learning is a pedagogical practice that places student learning at its centre. It focuses on *how* students learn, not just on *what* they learn. We as teachers need to encourage students to 'think hard', rather than passively receive information. Active learning encourages students to take responsibility for their learning and supports them in becoming independent and confident learners in school and beyond.

Research shows us that it is not possible to transmit understanding to students by simply telling them what they need to know. Instead, we need to make sure that we challenge students' thinking and support them in building their own understanding. Active learning encourages more complex thought processes, such as evaluating, analysing and synthesising, which foster a greater number of neural connections in the brain. While some students may be able to create their own meaning from information received passively, others will not. Active learning enables all students to build knowledge and understanding in response to the opportunities we provide.

Why adopt an active learning approach?

We can enrich all areas of the curriculum, at all stages, by embedding an active learning approach.

In active learning, we need to think not only about the content but also about the process. It gives students greater involvement and control over their learning. This encourages all students to stay focused on their learning, which will often give them greater enthusiasm for their studies. Active learning is intellectually stimulating and taking this approach encourages a level of academic discussion with our students that we, as teachers, can also enjoy. Healthy discussion means that students are engaging with us as a partner in their learning.

Students will better be able to revise for examinations in the sense that revision really is 're-vision' of the ideas that they already understand.

Active learning develops students' analytical skills, supporting them to be better problem solvers and more effective in their application of knowledge. They will be prepared to deal with challenging and unexpected situations. As a result, students are more confident in continuing to learn once they have left school and are better equipped for the transition to higher education and the workplace.

What are the challenges of incorporating active learning?

When people start thinking about putting active learning into practice, they often make the mistake of thinking more about the activity they want to design than about the learning. The most important thing is to put the student and the learning at the centre of our planning. A task can be quite simple but still get the student to think critically and independently. Sometimes a complicated task does not actually help to develop the students' thinking or understanding at all. We need to consider carefully what we want our students to learn or understand and then shape the task to activate this learning.

Introduction

Studying Business involves learning how to solve problems and make recommendations. Studying Economics involves analysing a variety of economic issues and being able to assess the actions that governments might take to improve markets. Both subjects require students to apply their understanding, analyse a particular situation and make judgements. Building these skills requires students to be actively involved in learning and thinking through problems for themselves. This chapter looks at how we can encourage active learning in our subjects.

Engage

The key to a good lesson is to engage students. Imagine you are teaching the determinants of wages. What if you showed students a picture of the highest paid sportsperson you can find and ask whether they can guess how much that person earns per day, per week, per year? Then show a picture of a nurse. Compare their earnings. You can then extend this to other roles: police officer, sales person, shop assistant, taxi driver, pilot and so on, and open it up into a discussion of: Which is the most 'important' job and what determines how much someone doing that job earns? Why are nurses typically paid so little for what many would regard as a very important job? Are top sportspeople really worth the huge sums of money they are paid? This approach is likely to get some discussion going!

Once the topic is opened up and students are thinking for themselves, you can bring in the theory to show how it helps the analysis.

The example above shows that it is important for students to see theories, models, frameworks, studies and so on as valuable tools to help them analyse something they want to understand. Presenting a theory and telling students that they need to learn it might well lead to an internal (if not external!) 'Why should I?' However, if they are already thinking, debating and pondering over a topic and you can give them tools to make more sense of it, you become a valuable and welcome resource. Theories and models need to be presented as a way of making sense of topics that students want to understand rather than something they have to learn for the sake of it.

LESSON IDEA 6.1: VISUALISING BUSINESS AND ECONOMICS ISSUES

Select a series of images to show how it helps the analysis and ask students to consider the business or economic implications. For example:

- In the case of oil, you could consider the factors affecting short-run and long-run supply as well as demand. You could consider the causes of changes in recent years and the impact on different economies.
- In the case of a container ship, you could consider global supply chains, the relatively low costs of shipping items by container, the impact of containers on world trade and access to supplies and markets.

Figure 6.1

→

Figure 6.2

Let students work in groups and comment underneath each of the pictures on the business or economic issues they raise.

Ask, don't tell

Telling students about a topic may sometimes seem the best option. It is quick, you know they have made the notes you want them to make and you know they have the 'right' answer. The problem is that if you give them a different situation and ask them to explain what is happening or the consequences of the change being examined, they may struggle to analyse it. In both Business and Economics, students are regularly faced with unfamiliar data or situations. What you need is for them to have the skills to understand what is happening and why it matters. Telling students about the specifics of a devaluation of a currency, for example, does not necessarily help them to think through another currency change in another economy. Being able to repeat what you have been told is different from understanding the principles and having the skills to analyse a different situation. The key to effective teaching is to help students ask the right questions and develop their ability to think through a problem through active learning. If students have to explore an issue and ask what they need to know to be able to understand, it is much more likely that their findings will seem meaningful to them. Providing activities that generate questions leads to a much more effective learning process.

Simply presenting an image or a situation and asking a question can be a very powerful way of starting a lesson. Some examples of impactful starter questions could be: 'Why do you think this has happened? Why do you think it is important? What do you think is the significance of this?'

You need a clear idea of what you want to get out of any activity and, for example, what notes you want students to have at the end. However, this learning journey can be driven by the students with you nudging, guiding and having the overview of where they are headed.

Imagine, for example, that you are considering factors affecting demand. Ultimately you know you want to get to factors such as income, the price of other products and marketing activities of businesses. You could just tell students the information; you could even give them a handout with the list written down, but how meaningful would this be for them? They wouldn't necessarily have thought about it, they wouldn't have had a chance to question or challenge, they wouldn't have added in their own perceptions (and no matter how many times you teach a topic, you can always be surprised by new ideas and insights).

What about showing students a range of products and getting them to consider the factors that can influence the demand for them? Select some products that might get them sitting up in their seats (Have you seen the price of a penthouse flat in a New York? Have you wondered how many burgers are sold every year?). From this, you might still end up with the same list of the factors but this time they have been generated by the students themselves so they have more ownership of the list – it is 'their' list! They also will have related the factors influencing demand to something they understand, or were interested in, giving the task meaning. They will have appreciated how these factors may vary in importance depending on the context, which helps them to develop the skills to analyse demand factors for unfamiliar products.

Teacher Tip

Know where you want to get to in the lesson. Work out the activity to get you there, but let students contribute ideas so that they can be involved in the learning process.

Don't forget the 'wow factor'

A tennis ball used in matches at the Wimbledon tennis championships in England is made up of materials that have travelled over 50 000 miles to create the finished product. Wow! Why is the producer buying materials from suppliers all over the world? What challenges are there for managing suppliers based globally? The discussion has begun. Look for stories, data, insights that have the 'wow factor' (see Figure 6.3) and then the debate will flow. The questions will be asked and you should have plenty of volunteers for research.

There are over 1.9 billion servings of Coca Cola sold every day. Every day.

Wow!

How can the company produce this much?

Why is demand so high?

What is it about Coca Cola that consumers like so much?

In 2008 Zimbabwe's inflation rate reached 231 000 000%.

Wow!

How could this happen?

How did this affect different groups within society?

Where can I find out more?

Figure 6.3: Look for stories that have the 'wow factor'.

Teacher Tip

Try to collect some fascinating facts, special stories and dazzling data to add sparkle to the lesson and get students to sit up and wonder. For example, few of us would fail to be impressed by the fact that if Facebook were a country it would have the largest population of any country in the world, and then we would start to wonder why.

Questioning

Questioning is an art which we all need to keep practising and developing. Questioning can encourage and develop analytical and evaluative thinking; it can build confidence and provide a valuable and exciting challenge for students.

However, poor questioning can limit thinking and fail to stretch. I have watched some lessons that simply asked students for yes/no answers and have almost shouted out 'Why?' or 'What if?' A student knows that interest rates can affect investment, but why? Is it possible to have low interest rates and low investment? Why? Don't lose this valuable opportunity to find out more about students' understanding and to develop their thinking further.

At its weakest, questioning invites one-word answers and you respond with 'correct' or 'good' and take it no further. You have learnt that one student in that room can recall an answer. You don't know whether that student understands the topic. You don't know if that student understands the causes and consequences. You don't know what anyone else thinks. You haven't helped students to develop their understanding. You have not helped them to reflect on their grasp of a topic. You haven't helped them to help others understand. Used well, questioning can help students build their understanding and get them really thinking through issues – you want to try to get to a moment when you can see from their expressions that they are trying to puzzle through a problem.

In one of my Economics classes recently, we were working on supply and demand. The following are examples of some questions that arose from the discussion about oil prices:

> **'What do you think will happen to the price of oil over time?'** It will go up.
>
> **'Why?'** Because it's running out.
>
> **'So what's happening to supply?'** It is decreasing.
>
> **'Any other reasons?'** We need more energy.
>
> **'Why?'** Demand is growing as countries grow.
>
> **'Excellent.'**

So now we had built on students' own understanding of why oil prices are increasing and helped them to see how this can be explained using supply and demand analysis. Students were happy, having worked through a problem and worked out an explanation.

Don't be afraid to throw in a few challenges:

'So why have oil prices been falling so much in the last year?'

At this stage, they may look a bit confused because this does not fit with what they have just argued – they have just explained why the price has been rising. Then you can see the real thinking start. They start to think about supply and demand. A falling price must be due to more supply or less demand. Why might this be … new sources? Slower growing economies …? Understanding is restored and lower prices explained. Now students have a big smile on their faces and feel very confident about their ability to cope with anything you are going to throw at them! So don't be afraid to challenge your students, to upset their understanding and make them really think about the complexities of the modern world.

Shake it up

Don't leave students sitting in the same seats next to the same people for the whole year. That just encourages the same thinking time and time again. Make sure they move around and work in different groups.

In a global world students may be changing teams, working remotely with people from all over the world and moving quickly from one team to another frequently. Think of the cabin crew on a plane – they come together for a flight and have to learn how to work with each other quickly (so they need to be trained to know what to do and how to interact with others). The next day, it may be a different flight and a different team, and they have to work with these people just as efficiently as they did with the previous colleagues. The same happens with management consultants, software developers, designers and many more jobs these days, where teams exist for a specific purpose and the membership changes as the task changes. School is as good a time as any to start getting used to changing teams and working with different people on different tasks. If we want new thinking, we want different perspectives, different approaches, different experiences, different insights so let's move people around and out of their comfort zone. Some businesses run meetings with everyone standing up to keep the discussion flowing. Why not set an activity where you do this with groups?

Teacher Tip

This is a good way of mixing up people into teams. Think how many teams you want for an activity. For five teams, for example, give students a number 1, 2, 3, 4 and 5. All the 1s move to form a group in one part of the room, all the 2s gather in another part, the 3s move to another part and so on.

Look for other ways of getting movement in the lesson. You could try 'Last man standing' to start the lesson – all students begin standing up and have to say in turn something that they learnt in the last class. If they repeat something that has already been said or hesitate, they have to sit down. The last person standing gets a prize!

Don't just use the board to display work, get students working on flip chart paper around the room if you can. Visibility is great – it helps students celebrate their own work, and it also means they know that what they do will be seen and commented on by their peers. This can be quite a motivator.

LESSON IDEA ONLINE 6.2: BRINGING MOVEMENT INTO LESSONS

You can use the approach behind this lesson idea for many topics. It is an excellent way of achieving active, reflective learning.

Setting the right task

If you want students to think and engage with their learning, you have to set them tasks that enable them to do this. I recently watched a lesson where students worked in groups and had to read and summarise a newspaper article. They spent most of the time they had been allocated reading the article independently – not really a group activity at all. There was no sense that each of the students had something to contribute and there was no sense of competition against the other team. It was a dull activity for the students.

Putting people together does not in itself create a group – you also need some shared activity and focus. What if the teacher had asked one group to present the case for a particular view (e.g. go ahead with the project) and the other group to present the case against (don't go ahead)? What if different members of the group had been given different pieces of information so they had to share ideas to piece together the big picture? It is likely this approach would have led to more buzz in the classroom and some genuinely shared learning.

LESSON IDEA ONLINE 6.3: UNDERSTANDING DECISION-MAKING

You can use this lesson idea to highlight how different people can bring different skills and experiences to a task. It is a good activity at the start of a course to get students thinking about the importance of objectives, strategy and decision-making.

Teacher Tip

Try to plan group activities so that individuals can each bring something to the discussion, rather than it becoming an opportunity for some individuals to 'hide' in the group and let others do all the work.

By all means prompt, question and nudge but avoid the temptation to lead or cut short the discussion. If you do this too often, students soon learn that you will do all the work for them. What's the result? They may become passive and not 'own' the lesson at all. At the same time, make sure particular students do not dominate and that everyone contributes to the discussion.

Summary

The key points to remember in this chapter are:

- The need to engage students in the subject. Try to think about the 'wow factor' and how you introduce your lessons.
- The value of active lessons. Make sure students are not just sitting passively and listening to you. Involve them in the learning process.
- It is important that students do most of the work. Your role is to be a facilitator.
- Good questioning is vital – use your questioning to assess and develop students' understanding.
- Use group work to promote collaborative learning. Students will learn from others and build on each other's skills.

Assessment for Learning

7

What is Assessment for Learning?

Assessment for Learning (AfL) is a teaching approach that generates feedback that can be used to improve students' performance. Students become more involved in the learning process and, from this, gain confidence in what they are expected to learn and to what standard. We as teachers gain insights into a student's level of understanding of a particular concept or topic, which helps to inform how we support their progression.

We need to understand the meaning and method of giving purposeful feedback to optimise learning. Feedback can be informal, such as oral comments to help students think through problems, or formal, such as through the use of rubrics to help clarify and scaffold learning and assessment objectives.

Why use Assessment for Learning?

By following well-designed approaches to AfL, we can understand better how our students are learning and use this to plan what we will do next with a class or individual students (see Figure 7.1). We can help our students to see what they are aiming for and to understand what they need to do to get there. AfL makes learning visible; it helps students understand more accurately the nature of the material they are learning and themselves as learners. The quality of interactions and feedback between students and teachers becomes critical to the learning process.

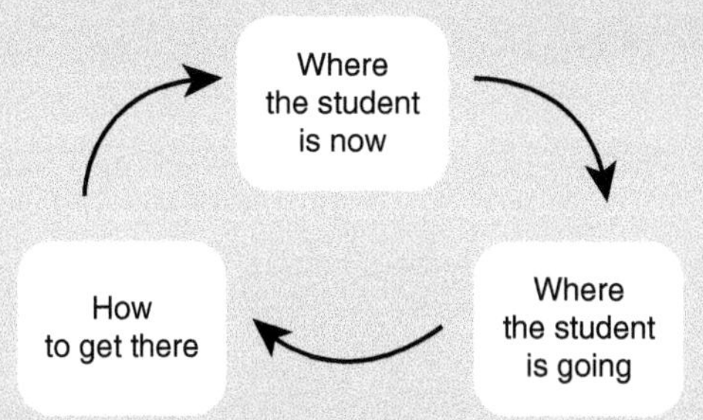

Figure 7.1: How can we use this plan to help our students?

We can use AfL to help our students focus on specific elements of their learning and to take greater responsibility for how they might move forward. AfL creates a valuable connection between assessment and learning activities, as the clarification of objectives will have a direct impact on how we devise teaching and learning strategies. AfL techniques can support students in becoming more confident in what they are learning, reflective in how they are learning, more likely to try out new approaches, and more engaged in what they are being asked to learn.

What are the challenges of incorporating AfL?

The use of AfL does not mean that we need to test students more frequently. It would be easy to just increase the amount of summative assessment and use this formatively as a regular method of helping us decide what to do next in our teaching. We can judge how much learning has taken place through ways other than testing, including, above all, communicating with our students in a variety of ways and getting to know them better as individuals.

Introduction

In Economics, students' understanding of markets and the economy builds as they go through the course. For example, they learn about supply, then demand and finally bring them together to analyse markets. It is important to know what students have understood at any moment so you can build on it or, if necessary, revisit areas until the understanding is more secure. In this chapter we highlight the need for and value of AfL and suggest some possible ways in which it can be done.

Remember what it is like to be a student

Think back to a conference where you have had to sit and listen for an hour. Did you fidget? Did you want to speak up? Did you lose concentration when what was being said seemed irrelevant? Problems occur if an audience is not engaged and no one is checking whether the individuals are interested or not; sitting and being talked at is not very productive.

As a teacher, you need to find out what students have actually understood, what they want to go over and what they want to know more about. If students have already understood a topic, move on. If some have and some haven't, set extension tasks for part of the group and focus on working with the others. For example, if some are busy analysing a topic, others could be evaluating.

Improving your AfL is an essential part of better teaching and is far more than just testing students or marking their homework. It is not checking whether someone has arrived at their destination; it is having a conversation throughout the journey that you are all on together to make sure that they and you know where they are going and how to get there.

Teacher Tip

It is not enough to ask whether students understand – they will say 'yes' to avoid you and them feeling awkward. Check the understanding at the end of each lesson with a simple set of questions. Assessments such as multiple choice, fill in the gaps or linking terms and definitions are quick and give immediate feedback. Alternatively, just ask students to rate their confidence level (red, amber, green) on the topics you covered in the lesson.

Explain to students why you are assessing them

Many students will fear being 'wrong' and worry about being 'tested', so explain the purpose of assessment – it is to help you understand what they know. It is important for students to think about how confidently they can answer questions, complete exercises and contribute to discussions; this is part of collaborative learning. You are not trying to catch them out – you are trying to work with them to help them more effectively. It is an assessment of **your** learning – so you can learn how to help your students – as much as an assessment of **their** learning.

A supportive learning environment

Explaining to students the value of assessment is part of building a collaborative approach. This also requires a sense that there is a supportive learning environment – we are working together as a team so we can all do well. We are here to identify how to improve, not simply measure, what students do or don't know. This sense that you are supporting students and that they should support each other will come from the way you talk to students, the nature of the feedback you give and what you celebrate (e.g. do you acknowledge those who try, those who rework their ideas, those who have identified how to improve and those who are resilient, as much as those who got the highest marks?).

Teacher Tip

At the end of a typical lesson, do you know how much progress each student has made? Or do you only know the progress of the few students who spoke? Think of activities where more students are engaged in producing work and sharing ideas, and where you can get a better overview of more students' progress.

How can you assess learning?

There are numerous ways that you can directly assess your students' progress. For example:

- **Ask five quick questions** at the beginning of the lesson to see what has been recalled from the last one. What has stuck in the students' memory? Why? What hasn't stuck? Why not? Have a prize for anyone who gets five questions right out of five! Think about what has worked for different students – they will have different ways of learning and the sooner you can identify these the better.
- **Mini whiteboards**. These are truly wonderful things. They enable very quick and easy assessment of everyone in the room. 'Show the effect of an increase on demand on the equilibrium price and quantity in market.' 'Use a break-even chart to show the effect of an increase in the variable cost per unit on the break-even output.' These sorts of tasks involving diagrams and calculations work extremely well using mini whiteboards. Use them to get students' ideas on how to approach a question. Ask students to write their ideas down and then you can compare their suggestions easily and quickly. It makes everything visible, so you can see what students are thinking without having to wander around the room to look at all their notebooks one by one.

- **Set tasks that lead to wall charts being produced** (see Figure 7.2). These are ideal if you want students to show the flow of an argument – for example, the effect of an increase in the exchange rate on the economy or the adjustment from short-run to long-run equilibrium in perfect competition. In Business, you could illustrate how an external change in the business environment might affect the different functional areas.

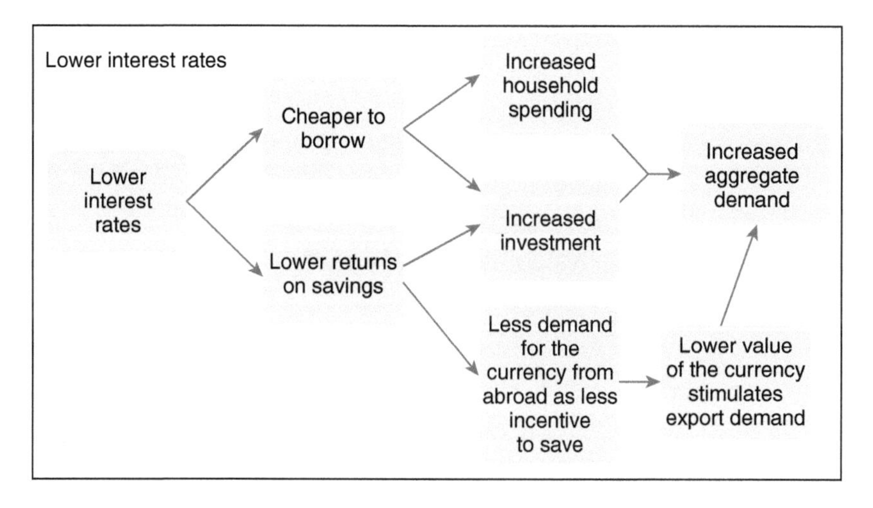

Figure 7.2: Wall charts provide an opportunity to highlight students' work and assess their understanding of a topic.

LESSON IDEA 7.1: PRODUCING A POSTER

Students work in teams to produce posters on a specific issue such as an analysis of competitive forces in an industry or the key economic issues facing a country. Producing posters can work well even for quite complex analysis. 'Is company X right to make a bid for company Y?' 'Should the government make reducing the budget deficit a priority?' Students have to communicate their arguments and the decision on, for example, one sheet of A1. Marks could be given for content, presentation, analysis and judgement and so on.

- **Multiple-choice questions.** These are a very quick way of checking understanding. Make sure that students explain to you or their classmates why they have chosen a particular answer. This can be very revealing indeed, and often what you might have thought was a 'wrong answer' has some very intelligent thinking behind it.

Q. Which of the following statements about a company is true?

A company:
a. has unlimited liability
b. is owned by the government
c. has shareholders
d. pays dividends every year

Now explain your answer.

Figure 7.3: Always make sure that students explain their answers even with multiple-choice questions. You will learn a lot about their areas of understanding and the areas where they need more support.

- **Role play**. Given that we learn best by explaining to others, why not ask students to put on a show to explain a topic to others? Alternatively, they could be given different roles to act out in a given situation. You could film these performances, but please do check school filming and consent form policy before recording your students.

Teacher Tip

For excellent examples of student-produced videos, watch 'TQM tea' videos that can be found on YouTube. While YouTube can be a useful resource, make sure to supervise your students to ensure that they do not access any inappropriate content.

LESSON IDEA 7.2: ACTING IT OUT

Ask students to act out a scenario to explain a key message. Provide a prop box for students to use. For example, in Business you could ask them to make a film illustrating how to motivate employees or an explanation of why cash flow matters. In Economics, what about asking students to make a film describing the problems of inflation or why a government might worry about monopolists? These videos will give you an insight into students' own perspective on a topic and how much they have understood.

LESSON IDEA 7.3: MEETING TO DISCUSS

A business is about to expand its facilities by building on an area of countryside, ruining the beautiful views and creating far more congestion but also much needed jobs. Write some background information on this for different stakeholders such as the landowners (some of whom want to sell and some who don't), the local council, the nearby villagers, homeowners worried about the traffic and so on. Give different information to different students, appoint a chair and let the meeting begin!

- **What did we learn?** Ask students what they learnt in your lesson today. Create a shared document (e.g. on Google Docs) and nominate a student to write up the key things that they learnt in the class. This does not mean repeating the notes but pulling out the key messages. Other students can add and comment on these points. This gives you insight into the main messages that came through from the lesson. Have they remembered the things you wanted them to remember? If not, why do you think this is? What can you change?
- **Questioning**. The way you ask questions is vital to your understanding of students' comprehension. Imagine that you ask a question and the student's response is not what you expected. If you are not careful, you simply move on to someone else until you get the answer you want. All you have learnt is that the first student could not answer your question. You do not know why. You do not know whether they can now answer it. Perhaps you could have stayed with their first response and tried to find out why they gave the answer they did. Perhaps you can go back to them once you have discussed the issue to see how they would now answer the question.

Teacher Tip

Remember: just because students are nodding when you explain something does not mean they understand it. Giving the impression of understanding can actually be a deliberate approach by students to avoid the difficult moment when it becomes clear they haven't followed what the teacher has been saying. Frequent, simple assessments that are not perceived as intimidating are vital.

Figure 7.4: Does this student actually understand what you have said? What can you do to check whether she has understood?

- **Tests**. You can, of course, use tests in the classroom and in an exam room to assess learning, for example mock exams under timed conditions based on the exam format. You can use past paper questions and the mark schemes to ensure that the feedback matches the assessment criteria exactly. When marking tests, think carefully about what you have learnt about the performance of a student a particular class and the whole cohort performance, not just what mark was achieved. Are students stronger in some topic areas than others? Are there certain skills they seem better at demonstrating than others? How is their timing? Try to pull out areas for you to work on as well as the students, following any test.

Teacher Tip

One of the criteria that inspectors consider when assessing a lesson is the progress made during the lesson by students. Sometimes this can be difficult to assess when observing a lesson. You can often tell how passionate, how enthusiastic or how knowledgeable a teacher is, but it is not always as easy to assess how much progress students have actually made in the lesson. If someone observing cannot tell, how can the teacher? Think about this when planning a lesson – it is not what you think you have 'told' students that counts; it is what they have learnt. A key question for you to think about at the end of a lesson is: 'How do you know what students learnt?' Think about what students can do at the end of the lesson that they could not do at the start. Can this be seen in the discussions they have had? The answers they have given? The exercises they have completed?

Providing feedback on written work

We generally place a lot of emphasis on written work and then spend hours marking it – but how effective is our feedback? It is worth thinking about what will be most useful to students and experimenting with different forms of feedback on their written work. Do students understand your comments? Do they read them? Do they take action as a result of it? One way to check this is to review with students, from time to time, what they are finding most useful in terms of feedback.

For example:

- Does it make a difference if your written feedback addresses students by name – such as 'John, this is a good piece of work because …'?
- Does it make a difference if your feedback is encouraging? 'Well done on the application in this response – you clearly researched well. Try to link your findings, such as the increased difficulties with

communication, with theory, e.g. diseconomies of scale', as opposed to 'You need to use theory more effectively'.

- Should you focus on one or two key strengths and one or two areas for improvement rather than have many different comments throughout the work? Should these be put clearly on a front sheet rather than within the piece of work where they can sometimes get lost?
- What happens if you do not put a final mark on the script? There is always a danger that students look at a mark and then switch off. I have tried putting no marks on work and seeing whether students can work out the mark given the comments made. This usually causes concern at first because it is not what students are used to. However, the response is generally positive over time as students start to appreciate that it helps them read the feedback properly and so see how to progress. Another option is to describe the skills and level achieved but then students have to match these comments against the mark scheme to decide on the mark they deserve. This is good for you as it helps to ensure that your comments match the grids in terms of the language used, and it helps students to engage with and actively look at the grids (not usually the most attractive of items), and think about the different skills and levels.
- How about if students put the areas for improvement at the top of their next piece of work before they start writing? This gives them specific areas to work on, and your feedback can focus on whether these areas have been addressed.
- How about asking students to summarise the feedback they get for each piece of work in the front of their books? They list the date, the task and the key areas for improvement. This is a very useful exercise that allows students to track what they need to work on. If the comments are the same each time, this is flagging that they and you need to make this area a real priority.
- Think about making feedback active; that is, it requires students to do something and not just read comments. For example, if you are worried about their use of terminology, you could ask them to define 'unit costs' or 'profitability' on their homework sheet. If you are worried about their ability to analyse, you could ask them to write an analytical paragraph as a follow-up activity.

Teacher Tip

Think about what you can do to ensure that students read your feedback. Do they summarise it in their own words? Do they add it to their next piece of work? Do they redo something as a result? One colleague used to include an unusual and random phrase in his feedback (e.g. 'the elephant often eats rice') and used to ask students to tell him what it was to check whether they had actually read his comments!

Other forms of feedback

Feedback does not only have to come from you. You should also be encouraging students to work together to assess each other's work and review their own progress (this is examined in more detail in Chapter 8 **Metacognition**). Get students to explain topics to each other – this is a very powerful means of assessment. A student will be able to measure his or her own ability to explain the issue to others, and the group can share their different insights into a topic.

Summary

The key points in this chapter are:

- It is important to assess learning regularly and not assume that material has been understood.
- We can assess learning in a range of ways – for example, through questioning tests and homework.
- It is important to think about the written feedback you provide to students and how they use it.
- You need to make AfL feel collaborative. Explain to students why they are being assessed and how it helps their learning.

8 Metacognition

What is metacognition?

Metacognition describes the processes involved when students plan, monitor, evaluate and make changes to their own learning behaviours. These processes help students to think about their own learning more explicitly and ensure that they are able to meet a learning goal that they have identified themselves or that we, as teachers, have set.

Metacognitive learners recognise what they find easy or difficult. They understand the demands of a particular learning task and are able to identify different approaches they could use to tackle a problem. Metacognitive learners are also able to make adjustments to their learning as they monitor their progress towards a particular learning goal.

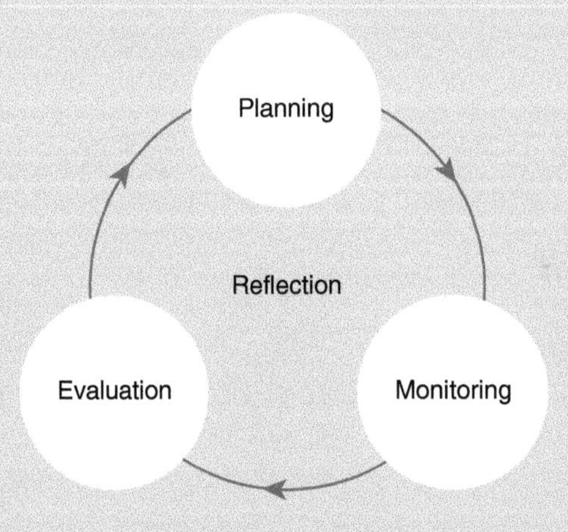

Figure 8.1: A helpful way to think about the phases involved in metacognition.

During the *planning* phase, students think about the explicit learning goal we have set and what we are asking them to do. As teachers, we need to make clear to students what success looks like in any given task before they embark on it. Students build on their prior knowledge, reflect on strategies they have used before and consider how they will approach the new task.

As students put their plan into action, they are constantly *monitoring* the progress they are making towards their learning goal. If the strategies they had decided to use are not working, they may decide to try something different.

Once they have completed the task, students determine how successful the strategy they used was in helping them to achieve their learning goal. During this *evaluation* phase, students think about what went well and what didn't go as well to help them decide what they could do differently next time. They may also think about what other types of problems they could solve using the same strategy.

Reflection is a fundamental part of the plan–monitor–evaluate process and there are various ways in which we can support our students to reflect on their learning process. In order to apply a metacognitive approach, students need access to a set of strategies that they can use and a classroom environment that encourages them to explore and develop their metacognitive skills.

Why teach metacognitive skills?

Research evidence suggests that the use of metacognitive skills plays an important role in successful learning. Metacognitive practices help students to monitor their own progress and take control of their learning. Metacognitive learners think about and learn from their mistakes and modify their learning strategies accordingly. Students who use metacognitive techniques find it improves their academic achievement across subjects, as it helps them transfer what they have learnt from one context to another context, or from a previous task to a new task.

What are the challenges of developing students' metacognitive skills?

For metacognition to be commonplace in the classroom, we need to encourage students to take time to think about and learn from their mistakes. Many students are afraid to make mistakes, meaning that they are less likely to take risks, explore new ways of thinking or tackle unfamiliar problems. We as teachers are instrumental in shaping the culture of learning in a classroom. For metacognitive practices to thrive, students need to feel confident enough to make mistakes, to discuss their mistakes and ultimately to view them as valuable, and often necessary, learning opportunities.

Introduction

Success in IGCSE and A Level Business Studies requires students to make decisions. They need to analyse a situation and identify what the key issues are and what to do next. Similarly, in Economics, students must analyse the causes of change in economic variables and make judgements on their implications or how to resolve economic inefficiency. This requires students who are able to think independently. Passive learners will not be able to deal with the demands of these subjects, which require them to apply their understanding in different scenarios. In this chapter, we consider how we can help students to take control of their studies and identify for themselves what they need to do to be able to have the knowledge and skills they require to do well in these subjects.

Managing their own learning journey

It is important for students to know how they are going to be able to plan what they need to do. This can involve:

Agreeing a checklist

One way of helping students to develop their own understanding is to make sure that when setting any tasks, the class discuss how it is going to be approached. For example, if asked whether a government should prevent monopolies, students can work in groups to produce a checklist of what needs to be included to produce an excellent answer. The focus here is not on the content but the process of producing an answer. The suggestions for the checklist from each group (such as the need to consider the case for and against monopoly, a judgement about efficiency and the use of abnormal profits) can be compared with the others and a list combining their ideas produced. This list can then be used by all students when producing the actual task. Students can literally tick off the different parts of their answer and check whether they have included the right elements.

LESSON IDEA ONLINE 8.1: LEARNING HOW TO ANSWER THE QUESTION

Use this lesson idea 8.1 to encourage students to practise developing a question and answer checklist to respond to a given question.

Reviewing exemplar work

You can tell students many times what is meant by analysis and evaluation, but it is usually much better to show examples of work and let them identify what is good and not so good in a response. We can then label it 'analysis' and 'evaluation' accordingly – but the most important thing is for students to recognise for themselves what works well and what does not. Being able to recognise a skill (or even the absence of a skill) is more important than just being able to name it.

Be prepared for students to identify the wrong things at first. They may choose the weakest arguments and think they are strong. They may value the long list of points against the developed arguments even though it is an 'analysis' question. They may not appreciate the need to be judgemental on an evaluative question. They may not pick up on the fact that the definition of gross domestic product or float time is not quite accurate – this is to be expected. So listen, let them discuss what they think of the exemplar work and gently guide them towards the true strengths and limitations of a response. Perhaps focus on a particular issue each time rather than ask for an overall assessment from the start. For example: How well has the response used economic diagrams to support its analysis? How well is business theory incorporated in the discussion of motivation? Over time, as students' experience increases, they will get better at identifying what works and does not work so well.

Teacher Tip

When choosing exemplar work, try to avoid the perfect response. If it is too good/unrealistic, students will spot this immediately and lose interest because you are showing them something that seems out of reach for most of them. Borderline or low-level A grades may be better. It is also useful to have mid-range work to compare and contrast.

When working through these exemplars, you should ask students to produce in teams an outline of the strengths of each response and also two or three ideas on how it could be improved. Stress the need for continual improvement and the importance of always reviewing how things have gone.

When looking at questions, try to get students to describe what an excellent response would look like. What about a good response? A reasonable one? A weak one?

Writing their own questions

Once students have gained a certain confidence in their abilities and are familiar with the format and style of the exam, you could get them to write some questions. Look at a news website and select a case study, such as a business that has just announced disappointing results. Ask students to write one analysis and one evaluative question in pairs on a given area of the syllabus. They can compare their questions with another pair, get feedback and then present their suggestions to the class. The discussion among themselves about what works and does not work helps deepen their understanding of assessment.

Being an examiner

It takes time to build the experience and confidence but the ultimate goal is for students to be able to mark their own work and the work of others. This means that they can identify skills, identify levels and identify a mark when they read each other's work. This type of exercise needs to be handled carefully as, at first, students tend to think that marking is *your* job. Don't be surprised if students are wary about the idea of marking other students' work – they will see this as requiring a particular expertise and initially will think you are the only one who can decide on 'the mark' that they should get. However, over time when you reinforce the idea of them taking control of their studies and progress, you can usually get students to appreciate the value of this type of exercise.

The benefits include students talking to each other about what skills are being demonstrated (such as application, analysis and evaluation), what level is achieved for each of the skills (e.g. is it a good or reasonable evaluation?) and what the overall level and mark might be. Let these discussions run as they will highlight areas of misunderstanding and areas where there is different understanding – all of which is useful to learn and move forward.

LESSON IDEA ONLINE 8.2: UNDERSTANDING ASSESSMENT

Use this lesson idea to develop students' understanding of assessment. You can use it on any given section of the syllabus.

Being a teacher

If students can master being examiners, why not get them to be teachers! The best way for anyone to remember and understand a topic is to have to teach it. Put students into groups, allocate topics and get students to present to each other. In lessons, you should have activities that involve students working in pairs and explaining to each other different aspects of the course. For example, you may have covered a topic such as fiscal policy or lean production and want to make sure that it has been internalised. Get students working in pairs, with one explaining the topic to the other in their own words.

Reviewing their progress with you

Find time to sit with students to discuss their progress individually during a term. However short the time you have to do this, it shows a genuine interest in them as individuals and sometimes you can address quite significant issues in a focused way. Sometimes students are reluctant to speak up in front of others but will do so on their own. To make sure the time is used productively, explain the purpose of the review, which is for students to discuss their progress and ask for support on any areas where they need help. Students can complete a review form. This could include:

a) What are my strengths in the material covered? Is my understanding of models such as the Boston Matrix or concepts such as the price elasticity of demand strong? Am I am able to apply this understanding to different contexts? Can I develop a line of analysis? Can I evaluate?

b) What areas do I want to focus on? For example, do I need to use aggregate demand and supply diagrams more to support my answers? Do I need to become more precise in my use of terms such as 'profit margin', 'unit costs' and 'total revenue'?

c) What will I do to develop these skills? For example, do I need to practise applying my answers more? Do I need to rewrite my tests? Do I need to read my notes more before starting my homework?

An individual review should lead to plans and set targets; these should be Specific, Measurable, Agreed, Realistic and Time-specific. They should lead to something in writing after a discussion with you about how to achieve them. Once the plan is set, students should then monitor their progress – this should be recorded – and then at the next meeting their progress can be reviewed with you. This will lead to an evaluation of the areas to work on next (see Figure 8.2). For example, they may have improved their use and labelling of diagrams in Economics and now need to focus on improving their conclusions.

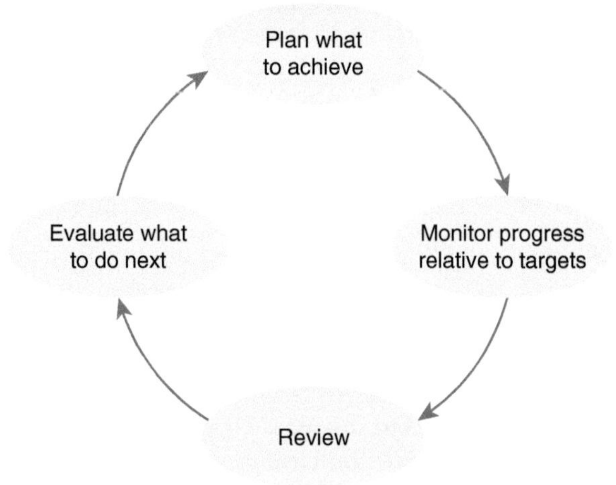

Figure 8.2: Students need to be able to assess where they are in their learning, decide what to do next and assess their progress.

Getting students to set and commit to their targets and getting them to think through how they might achieve them helps improve the level of engagement. These targets should be attainable and it should be possible to measure progress against them.

Teacher Tip

One useful technique is for students to list the topics covered and what they need to know for each section.

Students could create a sheet with the appropriate columns and then tick their level of understanding for each area. There could be a column where you can agree action to be taken on the areas where they are less confident. Many of us tend to do this sort of exercise towards the end of a course when we use it to shape students' revision. However, it is a good idea to undertake this sort of stock check quite regularly to gauge how things are going. Based on this, an action plan can be developed on how to improve in particular areas.

Here are some other ideas:

- Highlight the areas to focus on for each new piece of work. Students write at the start of a task what they want to focus on and what in particular they want feedback on. The area to focus on should be linked to the feedback on the previous task or an area discussed as part of a review. This is part of planning how to progress. For example, do I need to focus on more effective conclusions? Are my answers too theoretical and not using the context fully? Am I making lots of points but not developing them?
- Keep a list of assignments and the key feedback points. Both you and the students can then track whether the feedback is changing over time. If the feedback for five consecutive pieces of work refers to the need to 'apply to the context more', there is clearly an issue to address. Monitoring progress is essential, so that targets are not forgotten.

LESSON IDEA 8.3: HOW TO ANSWER QUESTIONS

Spend a lesson or part of a lesson on how to answer questions.

Give students a case study such as a takeover or a recent change in government economic policy, with some questions linked to it.

In small groups, students produce a guide to how to go about answering these questions. The guide should cover everything from the very beginning of being given the task to the handing in of the completed piece of work.

Things to consider include:

- checking the rubric
- planning their time
- reading the text, then the questions, then the text
- reading the question: identifying the command word and any other key points in the question that need addressing
- planning their response
- avoiding crossing things out
- reviewing their response if they finish early.

In the plenary, you can gather all the best ideas and produce a guide to taking exams. You might run this session focusing specifically on particular papers, and so end up with 'a guide to paper 1', 'a guide to paper 2' and so on. It could be a student assignment to produce the findings as a booklet, a short film or Microsoft Powerpoint presentation.

Making their own choices

I have seen some excellent lessons that have focused on students identifying what they want to know or which areas they feel they need to develop. It is so much easier for teachers to help someone who can tell them what they want to learn rather than to try to guess what they might want to know. Students leading their own learning journey, with the teacher as support, is much more effective than just teaching students what you think they need to know. Let's keep thinking of our lessons from the perspective of a student and help them control their learning.

Figure 8.3: We need to work with students to help them identify what would help them most.

Teacher Tip

When looking at a topic or exam paper, I tend to choose the questions my class is going to look at; for example: 'Let's go through question 5.' However, some might not need to do this and should be looking and thinking more about question 7 (which I have wrongly assumed that they can all do). So what about introducing a part of a lesson where students in pairs select questions from a list that they want to focus on? They work with their partner on trying to make progress – for example, this could be discussing how to answer it, doing some research to gather more information on it or reviewing the mark scheme to see how to answer it. They might then compare the work they have done on this question with the work others have done on their question.

LESSON IDEA 8.4: STUDENTS LEARNING HOW TO ASSESS THEIR OWN LEARNING

In advance of the lesson:

- take an examination paper (either a real one or one you have put together to cover the topics you have studied so far)
- produce a red, amber and green self-assessment sheet (see Table 5.1) to cover each of the questions
- students assess their own level of confidence
- take in these sheets and review them.

Based on this you can:

- identify the topics you most need to review
- identify which students are most confident generally and where there are real concerns.

Develop a lesson plan in which selected questions are worked on. Engineer the groups. For example, for the first 15 minutes you will be working on question 3, so pair up a student who is confident on this with one who is not. They discuss, then compare their findings with another group. Then change questions and pairings. Now get them to focus on question 7 and move them to work with new partners.

This highlights the fact that different people will have different strengths. It will create quite a sense of focus as pairs work on a specific project for a given period of time.

LESSON IDEA ONLINE 8.5: ASSESSING SOURCES OF INFORMATION

Use this lesson to emphasise to students the importance of assessing the sources of information they use.

Summary

The key points in this chapter are:

- The importance of students taking control of their own learning – this makes it more meaningful and helps them to plan the best way to make progress.
- The importance of students reflecting on their learning. You need to help students to develop the knowledge and skills to assess their learning and identify what else they need to do to improve. You want them to be teachers, examiners and actively thinking about what they know and can do as well as what they don't yet know.
- The importance and value of students as independent learners – this means that they have the skills and the right attitude to move on to the next stage of their academic career successfully.

Language awareness

9

What is language awareness?

For many students, English is an additional language. It might be their second or perhaps their third language. Depending on the school context, students might be learning all or just some of their subjects through English.

For all students, regardless of whether they are learning through their first language or an additional language, language is a vehicle for learning. It is through language that students access the learning intentions of the lesson and communicate their ideas. It is our responsibility as teachers to ensure that language doesn't present a barrier to learning.

One way to achieve this is to support our colleagues in becoming more language-aware. Language awareness is sensitivity to, and an understanding of, the language demands of our subject and the role these demands play in learning. A language-aware teacher plans strategies and scaffolds the appropriate support to help students overcome these language demands.

Why is it important for teachers of other subjects to be language-aware?

Many teachers are surprised when they receive a piece of written work that suggests a student who has no difficulties in everyday communication has had problems understanding the lesson. Issues arise when teachers assume that students who have attained a high degree of fluency and accuracy in everyday social English therefore have a corresponding level of academic language proficiency. Whether English is a student's first language or an additional language, students need time and the appropriate support to become proficient in academic language. This is the language that they are mostly exposed to in school and will be required to reproduce themselves. It will also scaffold their ability to access higher order thinking skills and improve levels of attainment.

What are the challenges of language awareness?

Many teachers of non-language subjects worry that there is no time to factor language support into their lessons, or that language is something they know little about. Some teachers may think that language support is not their role. However, we need to work with these teachers to create inclusive classrooms where all students can access the curriculum and where barriers to learning are reduced as much as possible. An increased awareness of the language needs of students aims to reduce any obstacles that learning through an additional language might present.

This doesn't mean that all teachers need to know the names of grammatical structures or need to be able to use the appropriate linguistic labels. What it does mean is that we all need to understand the challenges our students face, including their language level, and plan some strategies to help them overcome these challenges. These strategies do not need to take a lot of additional time and should eventually become integral to our process of planning, teaching and reflecting on our practice. We may need to support other teachers so that they are clear about the vocabulary and language that is specific to their subject, and how to teach, reinforce and develop it.

Introduction

In the first part of this chapter we highlight some of the strategies you might use to support students for whom the language and terminology of Business and Economics is new, and also for students for whom English is not their first language. We then consider the language demands of exams and how to build students' skills in these areas.

How can you help build language skills?

To help students cope with the language demands of our subjects, you need to:

- **Highlight the Business and Economics vocabulary you are going to use in advance**. Hand out a list of key terms to be used in the next lesson. Show the key terms on the board at the start of a lesson and go through them carefully during and at the end of the class. This is particularly important at the beginning of the course when you are trying to develop students' Business and Economics vocabulary. Watch your own phraseology and be careful to be precise in your use of terminology. Be careful not to switch between terms such as revenue, turnover and sales without making sure that students appreciate that they are the same. Be willing to repeat key statements to ensure that they have been understood and reword sentences to give alternative ways for students to access information.
- **Make sure that errors do not go unnoticed**. For example, economies of scale are to do with 'unit costs' not 'costs'; a price inelastic demand means that the percentage change in quantity demanded is smaller than the percentage change in price, not that there is no change. Don't let this sort of error go by without comment. Be constructive rather than critical but identify errors in spoken and written work.

- **Understand students' own learning backgrounds**. Find out as much as you can about students' points of reference. Discussing the approach of Facebook, for example, may have little meaning for students if they cannot access this in their country whereas Baidu might have meaning. Avoid using too many business and economic examples linked only to the country you are located in.
- **Be supportive**. Learning in a second language is a challenge but is also a great achievement. Praise students for what they are doing. Encourage them to try to express their ideas in English even if their expression may not initially be perfect.
- **Have regular vocabulary tests**. Research suggests that out of every 100 unfamiliar words that readers come across, only between 5 and 15 of them will then be learnt or looked up by the student. You need to intervene to help students develop their vocabulary and have regular vocabulary tests.
- **Make sure that students have a good Business and Economics dictionary** rather than a general one. Make sure that it is one that helps to put words in context rather than just defining the word.
- **Give feedback on students' use of language**. Whether or not English is their first language, students' use of Business and Economics terminology and the way they express their arguments are important. Give oral and written feedback on their progress in their area.

Teacher Tip

Set exercises to test students' vocabulary – for example, ask them to match the term to the correct definition. There are also free apps that students can download that are great for self-testing.

LESSON IDEA 9.1: USING THE RIGHT LANGUAGE

Produce sentences written in colloquial language. Ask students to translate them into the language of Business or Economics. For example: 'If no one is buying anything then no one has a job' might become 'If there is a lack in aggregate demand, this may lead to demand deficient unemployment'. 'The business makes a lot of money' might become 'The business earns a high return on capital employed'.

Teacher Tip

- Developing language skills does not just involve specific subject-related words. Problems in exams often come from students not understanding words such as 'implications', 'consequences' and 'limitations', so these types of words need to be explained and assessed as well. Look at past papers to collect a list of commonly used words in an exam situation.
- Work through Principal Examiners' reports to see the most common areas of confusion – for example, 'market research' and 'research and development', 'price' and 'cost'. Focus on these terms with regular testing.

Other steps to help students develop their language skills in Economics and Business

- **Produce a scheme of work showing what will be covered week by week** (and lesson by lesson if possible). Give this in advance to students so they can read ahead and prepare for the classes.
- **Make sure that students have enough time** for any task set. If you are reading an article, for example, make sure that students have

time to reflect and gather their thoughts – they are not just thinking what to say; they are also thinking of how to say or write it and need the extra time to do this.

- **Give students an easier book to read before they use the main 'textbook'**. For example, for A Level you might give them an IGCSE textbook and they can read this first on the relevant topics to get an insight into what to expect. Alternatively, give them a revision guide where topics are covered much more briefly.
- **Make sure that the language is clear when working through any articles or handouts**. Get students to identify words that are unclear in any article you give them before the analysis and discussion begins. Even if English is their first language, you will often find terms that are unfamiliar in the business press. Students can identify their own areas of uncertainty and compare what they know in pairs.
- **Provide cues** to help students make sense of what you are reading or discussing. If you are looking at a type of product, show an example of it. If you are discussing a particular type of business, show them pictures (see Figure 9.1). If you are discussing changes in economic variables, show charts of the data.

Figure 9.1: Provide visual cues wherever you can. This can help understanding.

- **Provide a variety of tasks**. One student may be good at listening to you in the lesson but not good at writing. Another student may be very confident in their written English but give the impression of having weak language skills in conversation. Look at a breakdown of a student's performance on the four areas of listening, speaking, reading and writing (see Table 9.1), and plan accordingly. Do not make assumptions about their skills in one area based on what you have seen in another. Use a variety of methods of assessment to gain an insight into their learning needs (see Chapter 7 **Assessment for Learning**). Look for different opportunities for students to show their talents by setting different tasks. For example, let them take part in a debate, make a short film about a topic or produce a poster on an issue.

Student	Reading score	Listening score	Writing score	Speaking score	Overall score
A	5/9	7/9	5/9	7/9	6/9
B	7/9	7/9	7/9	4/9	6/9

Table 9.1: Students may have similar overall scores in their English language skills but their performance within different areas could be very different.

- **Use rewriting exercises**. In Economics and Business, students need to understand the context of the question, which is often provided by some stimulus material. For some students, making sense of the stimulus material and using it as a basis for analysis is difficult. Set tasks that involve reading and summarising a Business and Economics situation in students' own words. Make sure that any handout has a blank line between each line of text – this way students can add in the translation of any term they do not know or make notes to explain this.

Teacher Tip

Set tasks that focus on students pulling out the key aspects of a given text. Use newspaper and business- and economics-focused magazines to provide the source material.

Select a range of sources to ensure that students encounter different terms – some may refer to 'shareholders', some to 'owners' and others to 'investors', for example.

Teacher Tip

Ask students to write on every other line when submitting written work or use wide spacing if typed. Doing so gives you space to make comments and correct any language issues.

The language demands of an exam

Having to think and learn in a second language can be difficult. An even more challenging task is to express your arguments on paper and address the specific demands of each question. Both Economics and Business require students to interpret questions very precisely and produce arguments demonstrating skills that match the assessment objectives. In this section, we consider the importance of command words and the particular challenges of the higher-level skill questions that require analysis and evaluation.

Understanding the command words

Different command words require different skills. To answer a question that begins 'Analyse', for example, students should produce a one-sided response providing logical chains of reasoning in context. By comparison, a question asking students to 'discuss' or 'evaluate' requires them to demonstrate judgement. Understanding these requirements leads to better answers and the effective use of time. It is surprising how many students waste time by producing unnecessary counter-arguments to 'analyse' questions.

Check the syllabus and the support materials on the Cambridge International Examinations website for a list of different command words and what is required for each of them. Explain these early in the course because they are fundamental to students. The meaning of terms may not be immediately clear, especially if English is students' second language. 'Discuss' may sound as if it simply requires you to 'write about' a topic, whereas it has to be evaluative. Give students written examples with a commentary so they can look over it in their own time.

Building analytical skills

Effective analysis provides a logical chain of argument that takes the reader from a given start point to the required end point. Imagine effective analysis as a series of stepping stones that take the reader from one side of a river to the other. Ineffective analysis:

- Does not provide enough steps to get you across. Often analysis is undeveloped and does not connect the start and end point effectively.
- Has steps missing (so you fall in). The logic of the argument is often missing.
- Has steps but they take you somewhere further down river, not across to the other side! For example, if asked 'Analyse the possible effect of lowering the price on market share', many responses would end on the impact on sales instead of market share.

Teacher Tip

Build language objectives into your lesson plans. How do you intend to support particular students? What particular language skills are you hoping to develop? For example, developing the use of the terms 'therefore' or 'as a result of' may be a target to improve analysis.

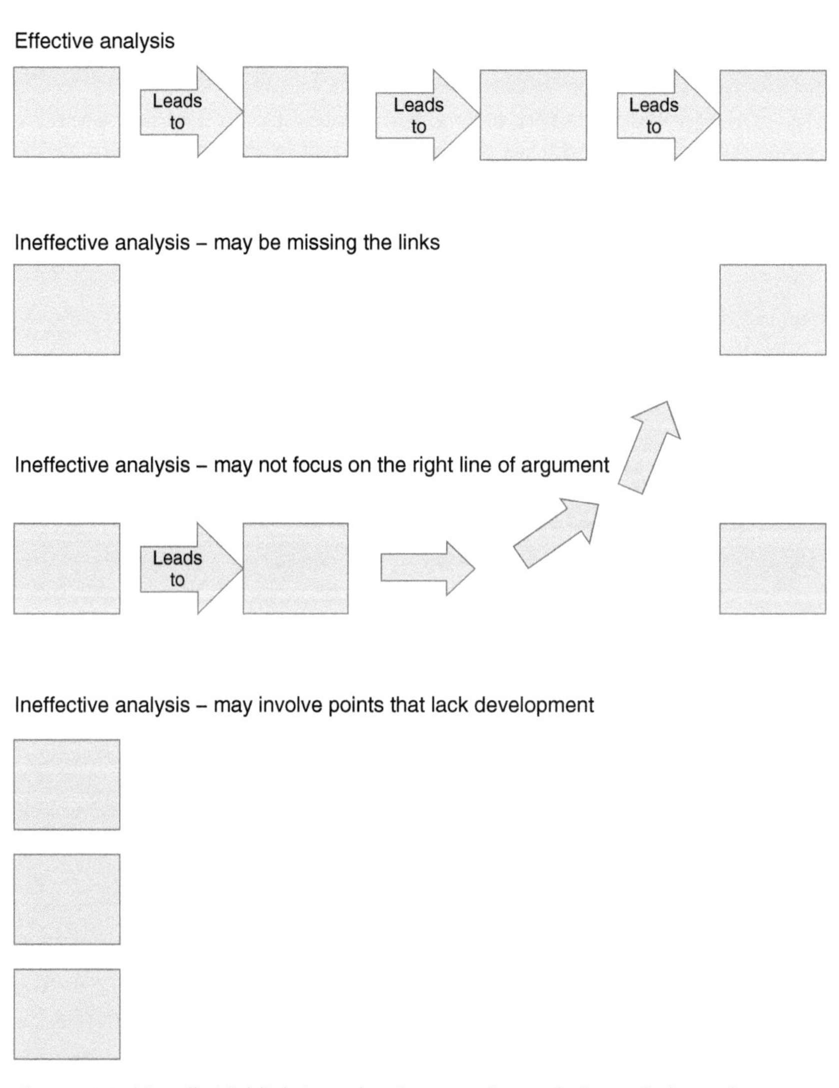

Figure 9.2: Visually highlighting what is meant by analysis can help students to understand what is required.

Teacher Tip

Look out for the word 'also'. This is often thought of as a way of connecting arguments by students but usually means that they are making a new and separate point.

Teacher Tip

Give students two answers to a question: in one there are two extended lines of argument but in the other there are just collections of points bunched into two paragraphs. Ask the students to identify (e.g. with a highlighter) every time a new point starts. This should show clearly the difference between the two responses.

LESSON IDEA ONLINE 9.2: DEVELOPING ANALYTICAL SKILLS

Use this lesson idea to help develop students' analytical skills and to make effective use of theory.

LESSON IDEA ONLINE 9.3: DEVELOPING CHAINS OF ARGUMENT

Use this lesson idea to develop logical chains of argument.

Building evaluative skills

Read any Principal Examiner's report in Business or Economics and it will refer to the need to weigh up arguments and reach a supported conclusion for evaluative questions. Good responses need to balance their arguments to provide a well-reasoned judgement.

The most straightforward judgements are deciding whether A is better than B. We need to highlight to students that this is what evaluation actually is, and that they do it all the time! The challenge is to move the judgement beyond assertion: we need to explain why A is better than B rather than just say it is.

You want students to:

- analyse the strengths of A
- analyse the strengths of B.

You also want them to consider the case for A *relative to* B. For example: A is better than B if . . . when . . . in these circumstances . . . because . . .

Many conclusions in exam answers are weak because they repeat the strengths of one option and ignore the strengths of the other option. This means that the structure is essentially 'A is good, B is good and therefore A is better'; not very logical.

A broader evaluative question might ask whether A is the 'best way of ...' or 'best solution to ...' This does not provide anything directly to compare A with. For example, if a student is asked whether decreasing tax is the best way to reduce unemployment, the student will need to select what to contrast with the tax cut – a reduction in interest rates; an increase in government spending; a change in welfare payments? The most common problem with this type of question is that students argue for the tax cut and then argue for a range of other options without comparing these with tax reductions. They examine a range of arguments but do not compare and contrast to make a judgement.

Again, showing visually what is meant by good evaluation may help, as in Figure 9.3.

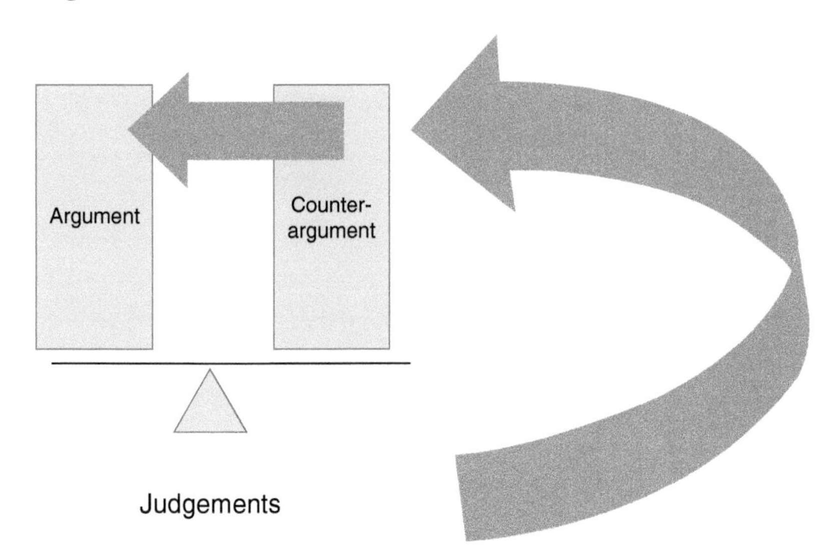

Figure 9.3: An evaluative answer is likely to have arguments and counter-arguments. The conclusion is built on the earlier arguments.

How can you help students with understanding the language demands of exams?

- **Use relevant command words** whenever setting work so students become familiar with them. Don't invent your own terms.
- **Set tasks where you change the command word.** For example, first start with 'Identify two factors that influence demand for goods and services in an economy'. Then change it to 'Explain'. Next, try it as 'Analyse'. Finally, change the question to 'Discuss whether X is the main factor influencing aggregate demand for an economy'. Students can reflect on what they need to do differently as the question changes.
- **Practise changing the question** (see Figure 9.4). For example:
  - **a** Analyse the factors influencing investment.
  - **b** Analyse the factors that may reduce the level of investment in an economy.
  - **c** Analyse the effects of a reduction in investment on an economy.
  - **d** To what extent are interest rates likely to be the major influence on the level of investment in an economy?

  Students can see the effect of a change in the emphasis of a question.

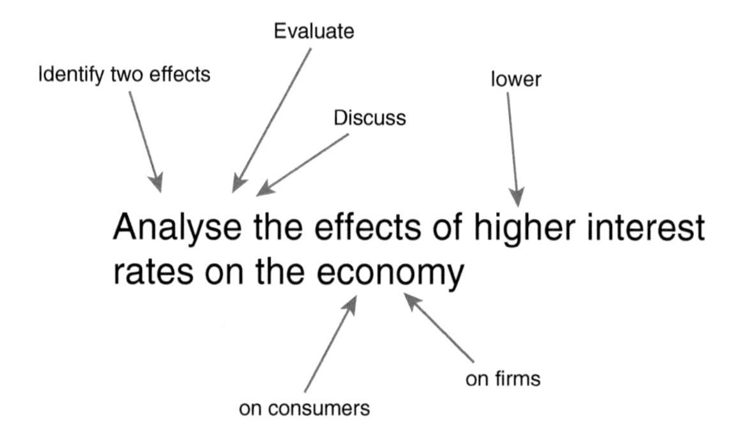

Figure 9.4: Ask students to change the question and discuss how this affects their answers.

- **Highlight it**. Ask students to review a response to a question using a highlighter to show the different skills (such as knowledge, application, analysis and evaluation) in different colours. This provides a very visual way of seeing how well the various skills are understood by students.
- **Ensure that students pick out the key 'context' words**. It may be that there is a 'sudden' increase in inflation, a 'major' fall in the exchange rate or an 'unexpected' fall in GDP growth. It could be a 'large' business, a 'multi-national' or 'public sector'. Good responses will pick up on these context words and appreciate their significance.

Teacher Tip

Set exercises for students based on the importance of words in the question that can act as 'hooks' for their arguments. What do they associate with these words? What difference does it make if it is 'private sector' or 'public sector'? What difference does it make if it is 'expected' or 'unexpected inflation'? And so on. Set exercises where you give groups a word and they brainstorm ideas associated with the word.

- **Set tasks in lessons with times for different stages of the writing process**. For example, set aside a significant proportion of time at the start to read the question without writing anything, then some time for notes but not actually writing a response, and lastly time to write their answer. This can help train students in the process of thinking, planning and identifying the key issues in a question before writing.
- **Ask students to check and highlight in their answers the terms used in the question**. If the question asks for the 'most important' factor, has this exact phrase actually been used? They may have argued about it being important but is it the 'most important'? Students often think they have answered a question but have not even used the terms in the question. Do the same exercise with analytical words such as 'therefore' or evaluative words such as 'especially'. How often do these words appear in the students' answers?

Summary

The key points of this chapter are:

- There is a need to build language skills for these subjects. Business and Economics have their own terminology and language demands, and students often need support.
- Students need to become confident in using Business and Economics terms and concepts accurately. This means that you should set tests, correct mistakes and practise using the right vocabulary.
- Business and Economics require students to show a range of skills such as analysis and evaluation. Students need to be aware of the demands of different command words and learn how to show these skills effectively. We have considered a number of ways in which students can gain a better understanding of the language requirements of these subjects and develop the confidence to demonstrate their skills successfully.

10

Inclusive education

What is inclusive education?

Individual differences among students will always exist; our challenge as teachers is to see these not as problems to be fixed but as opportunities to enrich and make learning accessible for all. Inclusion is an effort to make sure all students receive whatever specially designed instruction and support they need to succeed as learners.

An inclusive teacher welcomes all students and finds ways to accept and accommodate each individual student. An inclusive teacher identifies existing barriers that limit access to learning, then finds solutions and strategies to remove or reduce those barriers. Some barriers to inclusion are visible; others are hidden or difficult to recognise.

Barriers to inclusion might be the lack of educational resources available for teachers or an inflexible curriculum that does not take into account the learning differences that exist among all learners, across all ages. We also need to encourage students to understand each others' barriers, or this itself may become a barrier to learning.

Students may experience challenges because of any one or a combination of the following:

- behavioural and social skill difficulties
- communication or language disabilities
- concentration difficulties
- conflict in the home or that caused by political situations or national emergency
- executive functions, such as difficulties in understanding, planning and organising
- hearing impairments, acquired congenitally or through illness or injury
- literacy and language difficulties
- numeracy difficulties
- physical or neurological impairments, which may or may not be visible
- visual impairments, ranging from mild to severe.

We should be careful, however, not to label a student and create further barriers in so doing, particularly if we ourselves are not qualified to make a diagnosis. Each child is unique but it is our management of their learning environment that will decide the extent of the barrier and the need for it to be a factor. We need to be aware of a child's readiness to learn and their readiness for school.

Why is inclusive education important?

Teachers need to find ways to welcome all students and organise their teaching so that each student gets a learning experience that makes engagement and success possible. We should create a good match between what we teach and how we teach it, and what the student needs and is capable of. We need not only to ensure access but also make sure each student receives the support and individual attention that result in meaningful learning.

What are the challenges of an inclusive classroom?

Some students may have unexpected barriers. Those who consistently do well in class may not perform in exams, or those who are strong at writing may be weaker when speaking. Those who are considered to be the brightest students may also have barriers to learning. Some students may be working extra hard to compensate for barriers they prefer to keep hidden; some students may suddenly reveal limitations in their ability to learn, using the techniques they have been taught. We need to be aware of all corners of our classroom, be open and put ourselves in our students' shoes.

Introduction

Your role as a teacher is to aid the development of each student by providing an inclusive education so that all learners feel part of the process. This chapter examines some of the issues that students of Business and Economics might face, how you can provide the right sort of environment for them and the strategies you can adopt to make learning successful for all.

Creating a positive, supportive learning environment

In your class, there is likely to be a wide range of talents and all kinds of potential barriers to learning. For example, some students may find the following challenging:

- concentrating for long periods of time
- working on the more numerical topics in Business and Economics
- reading case studies or economic data in the time given
- expressing their ideas effectively on paper.

Get as much information as you can from specialists about the learning needs of your students as this can inform your planning and teaching.

There is likely to be a range of learning needs in the classroom – some of which may be acknowledged while others may not – so you need to build an environment where everyone feels involved and where recognising a challenge is seen as a positive thing rather than a problem. Praise those who identify something they want to go over or tackle in a different way, and those who ask for a different example of something. In many cases, the difficulties these students are facing may also be experienced by others in the class so it is good for everyone to raise these concerns. Work with students on finding solutions and overcoming hurdles. For some students, this means ensuring that they have additional resources (such as large-scale copies of handouts for those who are visually impaired) or extra time for those who are dyslexic. For others it is developing techniques to manage time effectively, developing structured approaches to help them organise their ideas on paper or developing strategies to help with the numerical elements of the courses. Ultimately, it is about developing an individual learning plan with each student, focusing on his or her particular requirement.

Teacher Tip

Time management is a useful skill to learn and will help students in their exams. For example, if the time available for an exam is 1 hour and 15 minutes, but students are advised to spend no longer than 35 minutes on one section, if they start the exam at 9.00 am they could put 9.35 am next to the next section to show when to move on to that part of the paper.

How can we create a positive, supportive environment?

- **Establish ways of working**. Establish the class rules when you first meet your students. Have a discussion with your students on how they think debates in class need to be managed to be productive.

  Establish individual ways of working. Work with students individually to overcome their barriers. This may mean extra time for tests, access to notes on the material covered, support materials or breaks during the lesson. Ask students what works best for them and build this into your lesson plans.

Teacher Tip

Ask students to produce their own guidance on how to work together and display the results in the classroom so you can refer back to them. Get everyone to sign the poster individually to encourage a sense of commitment.

- **Ensure that there is an environment of mutual respect.** Students are consumers and, in some cases, employees; they know a range of different businesses and are aware of issues in their community. My students know far more about some products than I do and we can all learn from each other. Do not underestimate what your students can bring to a lesson.
- **Encourage problem-solving and learning from each other.** Do not accept any behaviour or comments that make any other student feel uncomfortable. Lead by example. Highlight that businesses these days want team players – people who can bring something different to a team and work well with others who may have different strengths.
- **Introduce activities in which students can build on each other's strengths.** A good example of this is team-building exercises, which are often used in the business world. These can help build an environment in which everyone is supporting each other.

Teacher Tip

Many websites have team-building ideas on them, particularly in Business. Different activities focus on different skills and talents. For example, some need creative talents to solve a problem, others use numerical skills and so on. Select activities that are appropriate to your students and that will allow everyone to shine in some way in at least some of the activities.

Some departments have events such as 'Cake Friday' when students and teachers take turns to bring in cakes or biscuits for each other. Others organise a visit or activity near the start of the year – this is an opportunity for everyone to get to know all the others studying the subject and build a sense of working together.

LESSON IDEA 10.1: TRADING INTERNATIONALLY

This international trading game (found on the Economics Network website) is a superb way of getting students to work together, as well as providing a great starting point to discuss world trade issues.

- **Encourage failure**. Many great successes in business and in life come from mistakes. Rarely will an invention be successful in one go – it is usually a long process of trial, experimentation, error, rethinking and trying again. Developing our knowledge and understanding has the same pathway. It is not just what we know but how we got there and what we learnt along the way that is significant. When Thomas Edison was asked what it was like to fail 1000 times, he is said to have replied: 'I didn't fail 1000 times. The light bulb was an invention with 1000 steps.' Facebook is famous for having a culture in which it encourages employees to try something out and see what happens; if it goes wrong then stop doing it and try something else.
- **Create a learning environment in which students are happy to answer questions even if they are not totally sure**, are willing to ask for support and, if they do not understand something, are happy to admit it. If someone gets something 'wrong', explore why in an interested, supportive way – stress the value of understanding why it was not the answer you expected so that they can get it right next time. You will usually find there is some good thinking behind 'the wrong answer' – make sure you praise this. The business world these days is full of rapid change and uncertainty. Employers are looking for people who are willing to put forward ideas and questions rather than expecting people to know the answer. In some cases, people are not even sure what the right question to ask is, given the rapid change in some industries.

LESSON IDEA 10.2: THE MARSHMALLOW CHALLENGE

Use the marshmallow challenge, from the design projects section of Tom Wujec's website, to highlight the importance of being willing to try new approaches. The winning teams try things out, learn from failure and rebuild. Show the video and discuss the implications for your class.

- **Build the growth mindset**. The focus should not be on 'what I cannot do' but on 'what can I do to overcome any challenges'. Success comes from practice, not just innate talent. Great sportspeople work very hard at it. We need to work hard to get better but we can all improve. We should not classify ourselves or be classified as not being able to do something.

LESSON IDEA 10.3: PRACTICE MAKES PERFECT

Show students the YouTube video about Matthew Syed's 'Bounce'. It shows the importance of working at something to get better. While YouTube can be a useful resource, make sure to supervise your students to ensure that they do not access any inappropriate content.

Teacher Tip

Find out about the work of Carol Dweck and the growth mindset on the MindSet website. It is well worth exploring.

- **Think about the layout of your room**. I remember teaching in one room where every time I walked in, I moved the teacher's desk nearer to where the students' were sitting. Every time the next teacher came in, he moved it back again! For me, there was a huge gulf between the teaching and learning areas of the room. I wanted a sense of collaborative learning.
  Does the layout of the desks help learning and help to create the environment you want (see Figure 10.1)? For example, you might group the tables so that you have teams working on different activities. If everyone is in rows, it is difficult to collaborate. Alternatively, you might have a boardroom style set-up for presentations. Make sure that the layout suits the type of learning you want to have during that session. Changing the room layout helps show that the nature of the tasks is varying.
- **Think about your body language**. Make sure that your body language conveys an openness and a desire to listen. If you are frowning with your arms crossed when a student responds to a question, you are probably suggesting that you are not going to be impressed.
- **Think about where you stand** or sit in the classroom (and whether you stand or sit for most of the lesson is in itself a decision). I like to move around a room to get a sense of us being part of the process together and also to get a better sense of the room as a whole. You often spot issues such as an area of the room that cannot see the board or notice that the light shines on part of the board so it cannot be read easily. See what it is like from a different perspective – for example, how easy is it to read your writing from the back of the room?

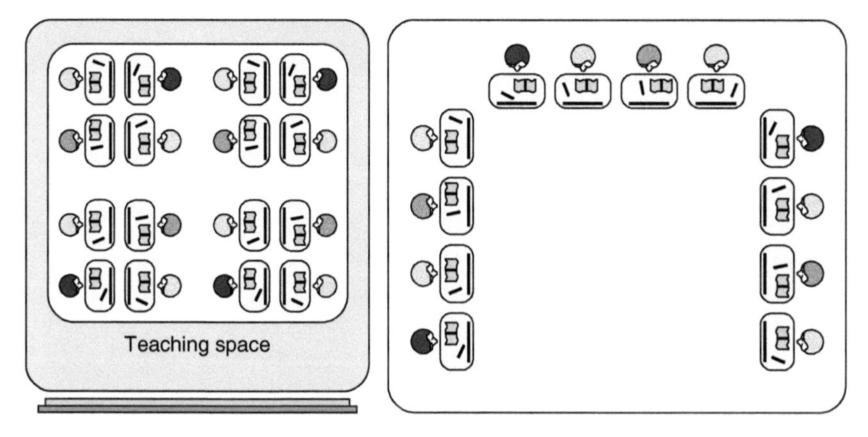

Figure 10.1: Changing the layout of a room may be useful for different types of activities: a) Desks in small groups: this might be appropriate for team tasks; b) Boardroom style: this might work well for presentations.

Strategies to ensure inclusivity

There are a number of potential barriers to learning in any class. We need to develop strategies to overcome them.

Ensure that there is variety in the tasks you set so all can shine

Given that students will have different learning styles and different strengths, you should make sure that there is variety in your teaching approaches and the tasks you set for homework. For example, some students will be much stronger orally than on paper. Some students will struggle to listen and make notes for long periods of time, and will respond better to tasks that they can engage with and where they can be more active. The key is to allow all students some way of showing what they can do to retain their engagement.

Consider the following ideas:

- **Having debates in class.** For example, should your country protect its producers against foreign competition? Is it better to be a private limited company or a public limited company?
- **Asking students to prepare and deliver presentations** (see Figure 10.2). This will allow students to show their ICT and multimedia skills. For example, you could ask them to compare and contrast the work of Maslow and Herzberg, or present the case for and against a higher minimum wage.
- **Setting work to be produced in different formats** (e.g. reports, blogs, short films or podcasts). How about asking for a report on the key economic challenges facing your country, or the case for and against a particular takeover deal in the news?

Figure 10.2: Involve and engage students by having them prepare and deliver presentations.

Differentiate by task

Assess where different students are in their learning and address this in the activities you set in class, as well as in the homework you give. For example, include extension tasks so students can move on to more challenging tasks, if appropriate. Some students might be showing the effects of movements in supply and demand curves on the equilibrium price and output while others move on to consider the importance of the price elasticity of demand and supply on these outcomes. Some students might be analysing the case for or against an expansion decision while others may be asked to come to a final judgement on whether or not to expand. Provide tasks which ensure that everyone is facing suitable challenges and you are not losing any engagement.

Provide structure

Having a clear objective for a lesson is important for everyone in the class but it is particularly reassuring to those who have specific educational needs, because it provides certainty and structure. It reassures, provides a point of reference and allows you and the students to measure progress – you can keep referring back to the structure, where you are and what is coming next.

Structure is also important when it comes to setting homework. If you can fix the same day each week for setting the work and a set day for collection, that makes a life a lot easier for students. They can then plan when to do your work and when to study for their other subjects. Make sure that the homework instructions are clear and ideally can be found online so that students can always refer back to what they have to do.

Think about your questioning approach

The way we work with students and the way we question them play a key role in the classroom environment. If we want students to take on responsibility for their studies, we must not be seen as the one holding the answers and trying to find fault with what they know. We must use questioning intelligently to help them on their journey.

- **Use your questioning to help students** assess their own understanding, to help them voice their ideas and develop their thinking. Make sure that questioning is used to help students explain concepts to each other.
- **Put the right question to the right person at the right time**. Gauge where a student is in their learning and what they can cope with happily by using a variety of means of AFL. Stretch students intellectually but build on what they know and help them gain confidence – don't destroy it.

- **Involve everyone in the discussion**. If you throw out open questions, you know the same people will often respond. This can be comforting because the eager students usually (not always!) know what they are talking about. The lesson has a good rhythm: you ask, they reply, you get the answer you want and the lesson moves on. The problem is that you are allowing less confident students to continue to hide in the corners while those who enjoy being the focus of attention get even more of your time. Spread the questions around more and don't allow anyone to dominate. Use a range of assessment methods to check where different students are in their understanding (see Chapter 7 **Assessment for Learning** for more information on this).

Provide additional support resources

- **Provide copies of notes for students** before or after the class so that during the lesson they can focus on absorbing the information. Some students are relatively slow at processing, so if they are busy writing notes they will not take in the content of the lesson itself. Also, struggling to keep up with note taking can add to their stress.
- **Put a summary of your lesson online if this is possible**. This can be done before the class so that students can prepare in advance and/or after the lesson and then review what has been covered. If students have resources in advance of the class, you can spend your time discussing/making sense of it rather than just transferring one piece of information from your head to theirs.
- **Provide access to more resources**. For those students you want to stretch, you might have additional reading that extends their understanding – perhaps particular newspaper articles, features in magazines such as *The Economist*, *The Economics Review* or *Business Review*, or articles by consultancies such as McKinsey and PWC. For those who need more support, you might want to give them access to more notes and videos. Some students may want to use laptops in lessons.
- **Produce copies of resources in different formats if required**. For example, provide large-size handouts for students who have a visual impairment, while some students with dyslexia might prefer handouts on coloured paper. Ideally, seek expert advice on resources that might be useful.

Teacher Tip

Look for achievements to celebrate –, not just absolute achievement but also effort, most improved, most resilient. Praise the student who rethinks how to approach a problem, who challenges a particular line of argument, or who supports another student well. Look for a range of learning behaviours to reward, not just outcomes.

Summary

The key points of this chapter are:

- It is important that you foster an inclusive environment so that the needs of all students are catered for. You need to adjust your teaching according to the requirements of different students.
- There are a range of strategies you can use, depending on the needs of your students. These include providing a clear structure to the lesson, providing additional resources and using questioning effectively.
- You need to make sure that the learning environment feels safe so students are willing and able to discuss any challenges they face.

11 Teaching with digital technologies

What are digital technologies?

Digital technologies enable our students to access a wealth of up-to-date digital resources, collaborate locally and globally, curate existing material and create new material. They include electronic devices and tools that manage and manipulate information and data.

Why use digital technologies in the classroom?

When used successfully, digital technologies have the potential to transform teaching and learning. The effective use of technology in the classroom encourages active learning, knowledge construction, inquiry and exploration among students. It should enhance an existing task or provide opportunities to do things that could not be done without it. It can also enhance the role of assessment, providing new ways for students to demonstrate evidence of learning.

New technologies are redefining relationships and enabling new opportunities. But there are also risks, so we should encourage our students to be knowledgeable about and responsible in their use of technology. Integrating technology into our teaching helps prepare students for a future rooted in an increasingly digitised world.

What are the challenges of using digital technologies?

The key to ensuring that technology is used effectively is to remember that it is simply a resource, and not an end in itself. As with the use of all resources, the key is not to start with the resource itself, but to start with what you want the student to learn. We need to think carefully about why and how to use technologies as well as evaluating their efficiency and effectiveness.

If students are asked to use digital technologies as part of their homework, it is important that all students are able to access the relevant technology outside school. A school needs to think about a response to any 'digital divide', because if technology is 'adding value', then all students need to be able to benefit. Some schools choose to make resources available to borrow or use in school, or even loan devices to students.

Safety for students and teachers is a key challenge for schools and it is important to consider issues such as the prevention of cyber-bullying, the hacking of personal information, access to illegal or banned materials and distractions from learning. As technology changes, schools and teachers need to adapt and implement policies and rules.

One of the greatest pitfalls is for a teacher to feel that they are not skilled technologists, and therefore not to try. Creative things can be done with simple technology, and a highly effective teacher who knows very little about technology can often achieve much more than a less effective teacher who is a technology expert. Knowing how to use technology is not the same as knowing how to teach with it.

Introduction

Digital technology is transforming the content of our subjects. Uber and AirBnB are completely disrupting their respective industries. E-commerce is ripping down the barriers to entry in markets such as insurance and clothing retail. The future of the car industry may now lie with Google rather than Ford. Digital technology is revolutionising the way people do business. The big issue with infrastructure these days may well be broadband speed rather than the motorway network. The key to communication with customers may be online, not print. We all need, therefore, to keep up with changes in technology because they are affecting what we are teaching. However, they are also transforming how we teach and the way students learn. In this chapter, we examine ways in which digital technology can help our teaching and learning.

What can digital technology do for us?

Digital technology can be very powerful in teaching Business and Economics. Given the focus on areas such as e-commerce in the business world, teachers should be eager to seize the opportunities this presents. Digital technology can:

- **Enable students to find information from multiple sources in different ways.** This can support the learning in your lessons. For example, students can work on a topic in your lesson, they can watch a video online on the same topic before or after the class and they can read notes online on the given issue. Multi-channel learning! Given that Business and Economics are constantly developing and there is so much in the news you probably want to incorporate into your teaching and learning, access to online resources is incredibly valuable. A topic such as takeovers or monetary policy may be outlined in a print book but this is really brought to life when students research an actual takeover in the news or can analyse the effects of a recent change in policy by a central bank. Students can link to news sites or blogs, and this brings home how dynamic Business and Economics are.

- **Provide superb resources.** To explain Herzberg's theory of motivation, why not get students to watch his video 'Jumping for Jelly Beans' (which can be found on YouTube)? To explain how Porter's five forces affect profitability in an industry, students could watch Porter's own explanation on a Harvard video: 'How the competitive forces shape strategy' (on YouTube). While YouTube can be a useful resource, make sure to supervise your students to ensure that they do not access any inappropriate content. The internet enables you and your students to access huge amounts of data – just think of the economic data available at the OECD, the CIA Country Factbook and the World Bank; or the industry insights that can be found from consultants such as McKinsey, PWC and Goldman Sachs.
- **Allow you to set different forms of homework.** For example, you can ask students to contribute to a blog or a vlog; this is ideal for building an awareness of contemporary business or economics events. Alternatively, ask them to make a short video to analyse a topic – you will almost certainly be amazed by the results.
- **Allow shared work.** Employers today stress the need to collaborate – students need to learn to work together and this is often online because colleagues are based all over the world. You can begin getting students used to this now. For example, they can create shared working documents (e.g. on Google Docs). This allows students to work on a piece of work or a presentation together. They can see each other's ideas and how their work is evolving together. They can all work on a task simultaneously and so get used to project work (see Figure 11.1).

Figure 11.1: Shared work allows students to learn from each other.

- **Allow you to have different forms of feedback**. For example, if you have the right software and interactive whiteboards, students can vote on various issues. You can also use surveys to get feedback (which can be anonymous if you wish) on any aspect of the course, such as the nature of homework, the value of different sources of information and different activities. You can find many free survey builders online.
- **Enable independent research for homework.** You can provide students with an area to research – such as a study of change management or of government economic policy – and they can search online for the material they want. This can allow them to access a much wider range of information than the textbook can provide. In class, students can also search for information to help answer a particular question. For example, you may ask students to decide on whether to invest in a particular company's shares and then let them research information about the business to make the decision.
- **Enable better tracking of students' progress and performance**. This will depend on what system you have but many virtual learning environments now have the ability to set tasks, have work submitted and save marks to a mark book. This can make life easier for you in terms of having easy access to student data and the feedback provided.
- **Help students revise.** There are many revision and resource websites and apps that students can use to aid their learning.
- **Provide better ways of communicating with students**. Are your students on social media a lot of the time? If so, is your department? Are you linking them to interesting articles? Posting comments on issues in the news? Whichever social media you use, this is an opportunity to engage students in your subjects. Our subjects are so relevant to the world around us and social media provides a wonderful way of keeping students up to date; and don't forget that the social media companies are themselves fantastic case studies.

Digital technology and your teaching

It is clear how digital technology is changing the way we shop, the way we learn about what is happening in the world and the way we communicate with others. How is it affecting your teaching? What resources are now available to you and your students, and how have you responded to this? Are there ways you can develop your teaching with this new resource?

For example, I have seen several teachers produce their own short videos on topics and post these online for students. Nowadays, it only takes a mobile phone and a small amount of time. The production quality can be basic but this need not matter; the videos themselves can still be powerful. Videos can be used to explain topics, to revise topics or even to give feedback on a piece of work or test. Students who did not follow something in class can revisit it in their own time, at a time and place that suits them.

Alternatively, you can find podcast software and produce podcasts for students. For some students, this can provide much more effective feedback than written notes.

Teacher Tip

For a good model to follow if you decide to make your own videos, look at the videos of John Kotter on change (you can find these on YouTube). They are simple and short but well structured – here is what I am going to tell you, this is why I think this and this is what I told you.

Treat with care

Digital technology gives access to a huge range of potentially amazing resources including websites, videos, blogs and podcasts. For those wishing to stretch themselves, students can even access university resources including some outstanding institutions such as Stanford.

However, digital technology also brings with it problems and dangers. One major difficulty is that, if you are not careful, students come to see collecting data as an end in itself, and the easier it is to collect it, the more they are likely to gather it. The result can be pages of downloaded notes, website links and source material that sit in a pile but are rarely used and that have involved no real analysis or critical thinking.

Know how and where to find information (and appreciate that information is different from data)

Students need to become e-literate. This means that they need to know which sites are good to look at and which ones are not. They must be helped to develop the ability to judge for themselves what is and is not a useful site. They must know which search terms are effective, how irrelevant sources need to be avoided and how to sort through their findings efficiently to identify what might be useful.

LESSON IDEA ONLINE 11.1: DEVELOPING E-LITERACY

You can use this lesson idea to teach e-literacy.

Summarise and analyse what students find

Students need to be able to extract the key points from anything they find online and rewrite them in their own words. Plagiarism is a major problem these days in schools and also in universities. Students often simply lift information from other sources and present this in their arguments as if it were their own. In many cases, this is due to a lack of awareness of what they are supposed to do rather than a deliberate attempt to mislead. It is, therefore, important that you practise exercises where students have to summarise and rewrite information that they find in their own words. It is also important to discuss why plagiarism is unacceptable – if they don't come across this as an issue at school, they most certainly will at university and for some it is a major shock.

Teacher Tip

One of the many benefits of the internet is that it allows people to gather alternative views very easily. This should help with your teaching in building critical thinking.

Take any view, for example 'protectionism is a good thing'. You can soon find an alternative view – 'the dangers of protectionism' – and you have a debate going!

Understand that simply because something is online does not make it true

While being a potentially brilliant resource, many universities are reluctant to accept Wikipedia, for example, as a source because the information in it is not always reliable. Companies will produce information that flatters themselves, pressure groups will promote their own cause and some sites may contain assertions without any evidence to support them.

LESSON IDEA ONLINE 11.2: ASSESSING THE VALUE OF AN ONLINE SOURCE

You can use this lesson idea to develop students' ability to critically assess the value of a website.

Digital intelligence and control

Digital technology can be powerful and empower students if used well. It highlights that our role as teachers is to help direct, facilitate and guide. Teachers are no longer the 'holders of knowledge' – students can access all teachers know and more. You need to give them the skills to do this and build their digital intelligence (see Figure 11.2).

Figure 11.2: Students can use digital technology in the lesson to research and produce presentations.

For example, I have seen laptops used very effectively in lessons by students who prefer to work this way. They can save their notes, and where appropriate they can search online for information that contributes to the lesson. The same is true of mobile phones. I have seen some excellent classes where students 'bring their own device' and use phones as part of the class to find information and research an issue from different perspectives (e.g. you could take an issue such as zero hours contracts and guide different students to a variety of sites to get a range of perspectives). This can be a dynamic lesson that feels active to students and is a great example of shared learning.

However, you do need to control how the technology is used and you need to frame your tasks. The danger is that students using laptops in class may end up looking at their own sites and you cannot easily tell this from the front of the class (so establish the rule at the beginning of the year that they search only for what you ask them to search for, and keep moving around to see the screens!). In addition, there is a danger that if they bring mobile phones or tablets into class, they will be distracted by social media. So by all means have lessons where students are online and feeding into the lesson, but this method needs to be monitored.

Teacher Tip

Ask students to rate the resources they use. Point students in the direction of a number of news, business magazine and student resource websites. Ask them to write a review of each one and perhaps give it a star rating. Put these reviews in a shared document online so students can add to each other's comments, and you will have an overall star rating and review of a site.

LESSON IDEA 11.3: RESEARCHING ONLINE

Identify a key business or economics story in the press at the moment. Ask students to research the story from four different sources. They should compare and contrast the way these sources have covered the story.

Is the data the same? Is the interpretation of, for example, the causes and consequences the same? If there are differences, why do they exist?

Students should then rate the sites in terms of the perceived reliability (from 0 – not very reliable to 5 – very reliable). They should explain their judgements.

IT is a resource, not a cure

Digital technology is a resource – it is not a cure for everything.

- You cannot just point students at the internet and let them roam free! They will get lost and overwhelmed. There is simply too much information there at all sorts of levels, and you need to help them define their main search areas so they have a comfort zone.
- You cannot simply give students access to revision websites and assume that they will revise! They might, they might not, but there are ways in which you can add value. By all means, let them study topics online or revise online but use this to enable you to develop teaching plans around this. If more work is done outside of the classroom, this leaves you free to focus on the real value added of stretching those that need stretching and supporting those that need supporting.
- You cannot use watching online videos as a means to keep students occupied! Videos can break up a lesson wonderfully. They can often illustrate a topic better than a teacher can; they reinforce some of the messages and they can bring moments of magic. However, you need to prepare properly so you know which parts you are using and what students are meant to learn from watching the video. For example, you might have a worksheet for them to complete as they watch the film.

Teacher Tip

Figure 11.3

If you haven't come across the Invisible Gorilla video (on the Invisible Gorilla website), you and your students are in for a treat. It is an amazing way of highlighting why sometimes managers miss the obvious. It's easy to look back at business failure and struggle to understand why they didn't realise they were headed for disaster. This video helps explain why it is not so easy to spot things at the time, and shows how you can miss events that seem so obvious when you look back.

For good teaching, you need to develop a positive learning environment for your students, you need to make learning active, and you need to be the guide, the adviser and the facilitator. Digital technology can help you to do all this but it still needs to be thought through. Don't assume that having better technology guarantees better teaching. I have seen classrooms equipped with fantastic electronic whiteboards but these have been used in pretty much the same way as a traditional whiteboard – this is a waste of a great opportunity to use technology effectively. At the same time, it is easy to get carried away with technology and have a lesson so full of videos, interactive quizzes and whiteboard activities that the actual learning is lost.

Teacher Tip

There are many different sites, and what works will vary from region to region. In the UK one of the best sources is the BBC.

If you want a list and brief description of different sites, you can visit the Economics and Business Association website.

Summary

The key points of this chapter are:

- The impact of digital technology on teaching and learning in our subjects. The changes being made in technology provide teachers with a tremendous opportunity to develop and improve teaching. Digital technology provides many more resources for teachers and for students. It also provides you with new ways of teaching and assessing progress.
- The challenges that digital technology can bring. You need to think about how digital technology can benefit the way you deliver the subjects, and adapt to the needs of students. You also need to think how it helps students plan their journey. However, you need to avoid an assumption that using technology will necessarily improve the teaching and learning; you need to be selective, creative and thoughtful in the use of this resource.

12 Global thinking

What is global thinking?

Global thinking is about learning how to live in a complex world as an active and engaged citizen. It is about considering the bigger picture and appreciating the nature and depth of our shared humanity.

When we encourage global thinking in students we help them recognise, examine and express their own and others' perspectives. We need to scaffold students' thinking to enable them to engage on cognitive, social and emotional levels, and construct their understanding of the world to be able to participate fully in its future.

We as teachers can help students develop routines and habits of mind to enable them to move beyond the familiar, discern that which is of local and global significance, make comparisons, take a cultural perspective and challenge stereotypes. We can encourage them to learn about contexts and traditions, and provide opportunities for them to reflect on their own and others' viewpoints.

Why adopt a global thinking approach?

Global thinking is particularly relevant in an interconnected, digitised world where ideas, opinions and trends are rapidly and relentlessly circulated. Students learn to pause and evaluate. They study why a topic is important on a personal, local and global scale, and they will be motivated to understand the world and their significance in it. Students gain a deeper understanding of why different viewpoints and ideas are held across the world.

Global thinking is something we can nurture both within and across disciplines. We can invite students to learn how to use different lenses from each discipline to see and interpret the world. They also learn how best to apply and communicate key concepts within and across disciplines. We can help our students select the appropriate media and technology to communicate and create their own personal synthesis of the information they have gathered.

Global thinking enables students to become more rounded individuals who perceive themselves as actors in a global context and who value diversity. It encourages them to become more aware, curious and interested in learning about the world and how it works. It helps students to challenge assumptions and stereotypes, to be better informed and more respectful. Global thinking takes the focus beyond exams and grades, or even checklists of skills and attributes. It develops students who are more ready to compete in the global marketplace and more able to participate effectively in an interconnected world.

What are the challenges of incorporating global thinking?

The pressures of an already full curriculum, the need to meet national and local standards, and the demands of exam preparation may make it seem challenging to find time to incorporate global thinking into lessons and programmes of study. A whole-school approach may be required for global thinking to be incorporated in subject plans for teaching and learning.

We need to give all students the opportunity to find their voice and participate actively and confidently, regardless of their background and world experiences, when exploring issues of global significance. We need to design suitable activities that are clear, ongoing and varying. Students need to be able to connect with materials, and extend and challenge their thinking. We also need to devise and use new forms of assessment that incorporate flexible and cooperative thinking.

Introduction

We live in a complex world in which businesses have global supply chains, sell their products all over world and often recruit staff from many countries. Economies are closely interrelated, as the domino effect of the 2008 financial crisis showed. In this chapter, we consider how you can develop global thinking in your students.

The global lens

Do you look at the world through a global lens? Or perhaps, like me, you may have got used to teaching certain topics in a way that can sometimes be a little parochial. Part of becoming more global in our outlook is to know more about what happens elsewhere but also it is a question of reviewing the global aspects of everything we teach.

Figure 12.1: The global lens.

LESSON IDEA 12.1: HOW MUCH DO WE KNOW ABOUT THE WORLD?

Ask your students in teams to estimate and illustrate the following.

If this class were the whole world, how many of you would be:

- women
- from Africa
- from Asia
- aged 15–25?
- earning more than $30,000 a year

and so on ...

This can be quite an interesting way to start comparing ideas and understanding about the world as a whole. In Business it is easy to think of the domestic market and not appreciate how different international markets can be, for example, in terms of income, family size, population numbers and age distribution.

I have taught externalities for many years but only discussed with students the issues that these market failures can create across borders relatively recently. Pollution generated in one country can impose costs on nearby countries, so how do we regulate or tax for this? And what about public goods? In Economics, I am used to discussing the lighthouse example, but may not have highlighted that the benefits are global – ships and passengers from all over the world benefit. I have taught property rights in the context of neighbours arguing over noise, but what about inter-country disputes over fishing rights? I have taught changes in costs and demand too many times to mention, but am now focusing more on the global changes that might have caused these shifts.

Some topics naturally lend themselves to global analysis – trade, exchange rates, entering overseas markets are obvious examples. It would be difficult to teach these without a global lens. However, there are many other topics we might have taught in a more inward-looking way in the past. Why not add a 'globalisation' box in your scheme of work or your lesson plan? Review all of your topics with your global lens to see how you can enhance your delivery. When analysing issues, you might want to address specifically the differences in the impact from a local, national and global perspective.

Teaching Tip

Use the idea of a global lens or global glasses in lessons. Perhaps produce an image to represent 'global glasses' and, where appropriate, ask students to pretend they are putting on their global glasses to see the given topic from this perspective.

For example, you could use the grid in Table 12.1 to help students to think beyond their local region when teaching PEST analysis.

	Local factors	National factors	Global factors
Political			
Economic			
Social			
Technological			

Table 12.1: Taking PEST analysis beyond the local region.

Once you have the global lens firmly fixed to your outlook on Business and Economics, it will influence all aspects of your teaching. When asking questions in class, setting homework or reading, you can check that you have added in the global perspective. For example:

- We often examine the impact of interest rate changes on our own economy, but how might they also affect other countries?
- We typically analyse exchange rate changes in relation to our exporters and importers and our own trade position, but what is the effect of a change in our exchange rate abroad? If the dollar strengthens against the yen, then the yen has weakened against the dollar is a truism but highlights all too well the interrelated nature of business and economies.

Asking for a global consideration of any analysis makes a useful extension activity.

LESSON IDEA 12.2: RESEARCHING EXPORTS AND IMPORTS

If we want students to think globally, a good starting point is the relationship between their country and the rest of the world.

Ask your students to research areas such as your country's:

- main export goods and services – and the regions it sells to
  - What proportion of the country's income is from exports and imports?
- main imported goods and services – and which regions it buys from
  - What are the country's biggest companies? What do they produce?

Working in teams, students should be able to produce some very good displays to illustrate your country's place in the world.

LESSON IDEA 12.3: INTERNATIONAL SUPPLIERS

Figure 12.2

Apple uses over 100 suppliers for parts for its iPhones. These are located all over the world. Search online for 'where are Apple products made?' and follow the link to the Mac World website.

Give students the list shown in the article and a map of the world.

They should plot on the map any country mentioned as a production location in the list shown.

Working in groups, students should address the following:

- Analyse the possible problems of working with suppliers based in different countries.
- Analyse why Apple uses other manufacturers rather than producing these items itself.

Use the news

Business and Economics are living, evolving subjects. What might be a key issue at one moment in the business world and economic environment is likely to be replaced by another issue the next day. The study of these subjects is intended to help students engage with the world around them and make more sense of it. It is important that you bring the world into your classroom (and, if possible, take your classroom to the world around you through visits). I always try to refer to issues in the news as part of each lesson to show how what we are studying is relevant and to check whether students are using their understanding to interpret events around them.

When looking for real world issues, try to think of the global perspective. What is the big economic story at the moment anywhere in the world? How might it affect your economy? What is the impact on local businesses? What is the big business issue at the moment? How is this relevant to business within your region? Always look for opportunities to link the global changes to the regional effects. And vice versa – what is happening locally, and how does this link to global economies and business? The links students will uncover will be fascinating and highlight, for example, the interrelatedness of businesses and economies. An earthquake in Japan may halt supplies of car parts around the world and limit sales. Bad weather in one part of the world may affect crops and prices, affecting inflation in countries around the globe.

Teaching Tip

You could have a 'Global issues' noticeboard or online space where students are expected to post stories. This could be a task given to a different student each week to find a story, or a homework for everyone. The key is to link the global event back to its local impact. Another option is to start a blog where students write up stories and comment on each other's work.

LESSON IDEA ONLINE 12.4: UNDERSTANDING DIFFERENT ECONOMIES

Use this lesson idea to help students consider economic issues around the world, and compare and contrast the most relevant issues in different regions.

Research

Developing a global perspective can be helped enormously through research tasks. Students can gather evidence to help compare and contrast what is happening around the world. This will help build important skills for university and careers. Whenever you are studying a topic, think about how students might research around it. For example, in macro-economics, what are unemployment rates, inflation rates, average income per person in different countries? How does this compare with your country? Why might there be differences?

A great deal of assessment is still in the form of essays and yet business people and economists are far more likely to write reports. So perhaps set reports for students to write with a global aspect. These could be on a particular issue such as the challenges of entering an overseas market, or a broader theme such as 'To what extent is greater globalisation desirable?'

LESSON IDEA ONLINE 12.5: THE SOURCE IS A RESOURCE

When doing your own research or setting research tasks for students, think about the sources you expect them to use. We can encourage students to use the websites of the big newspapers around the globe. Choose a particular day or week, allocate different students to different news sites around the globe and ask them to summarise the key business/economics story. It is fascinating to see that what might be dominating the news in our country may not even get a mention elsewhere (see Figure 12.3).

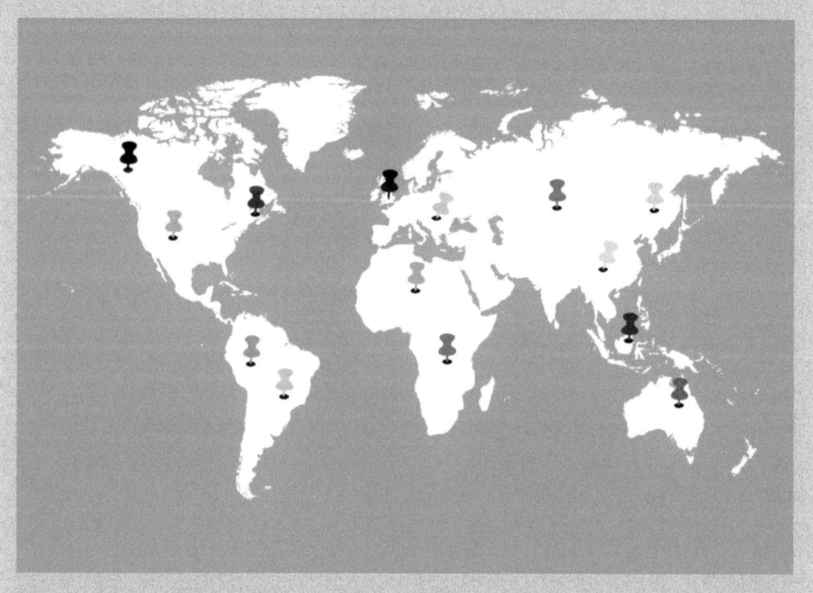

Figure 12.3: Give students a range of countries and ask them to find out the most recent business or economics story in that country.

LESSON IDEA 12.6: WHAT'S NEW?

Allocate students a particular country each. Ask them to research a business or economics story that is current in that country. They can then write a short report on the issue as homework.

You might produce a template for them to complete:

- country
- date
- summary of issue/event
- short analysis of the event/issues (e.g. why it occurred or the consequences)
- relevant business or economic concepts (e.g. price elasticity and capacity utilisation).

Students bring in their research, which can be displayed or saved online.

Let the debate begin

Globalisation is full of controversy. Is it a good thing? Why? What problems can it bring? Are there winners and losers? Who are they? Does it need to be regulated? Can it be?

To raise awareness of such issues, a debate is an excellent forum. Students can research different aspects of an issue and debate the case for and against. This helps to build evaluative skills and develop students' ability to look at issues from a different perspective. You may wish to run the debate formally following debating rules. Examples of debating society rules can be found on the Cambridge Union Society website.

Figure 12.4: Global issues provide opportunity for debates in the classroom.

Examples of possible debates include:

- Is there a multinational business about to locate in your region? Should you welcome it setting up or resist? Why?
- Many developed economies want emerging economies to grow more slowly to limit the pollution they create. Is this fair?
- Globalisation means that one product can be sold worldwide. Discuss.
- Is your country a member of a trade agreement? Are there any other countries that are thinking of joining? What are the implications for both countries?

Use your resources: students, families and friends

When teaching Business and Economics, you are probably looking to link the subject to students' own experiences – for example, how the theories of human resource management compare with students' own experiences of part-time work, and how brand-conscious they are.

You are also probably used to using their contacts – parents, friends and friends of friends – to come in and talk, and to help organise visits. This is true throughout the course and is also appropriate for the global context – do any of your students have a relation who has worked abroad and would be happy to come in and talk about this? Do they have any relations who work in businesses who export or import? Would they be able to come in and discuss the issues involved in international business? Remember to extend your speaker programme, broaden your question and answer session and, when talking to potential speakers, don't forget to think of the global aspect of their topic.

Working with others

One of the benefits of globalisation is the opportunity to work with others with different perspectives. We can all gain from a different set of eyes on a problem, particularly if they might look at the world differently. Look at this picture (Figure 12.5). What do you see – a rabbit or a duck?

Figure 12.5: There are many optical illusions, which can highlight how sometimes we do not see all there is to see. (For more examples of optical illusions, visit the Math World website.)

Such illusions highlight how we might see some things but not everything. They show the value that other people's perspectives can bring. This is true in terms of using the ideas and experiences of others in our class, but think how powerful it can be to harness the insights and perspectives of people from all over the world. However, we also need to be sensitive to the cultures and different viewpoints that people hold, and appreciate that at times this can lead to misunderstandings.

LESSON IDEA ONLINE 12.7: CULTURAL DIFFERENCES

Use this lesson idea to highlight how perspectives can vary across the world, and the benefits this can bring when solving a problem and thinking about business and economics issues.

LESSON IDEA 12.8: GLOBALISATION

Students research definitions of 'globalisation'. This can be done in the lesson or in advance of the class.

Compare the definitions – what are the similarities and differences? What is the significance of these differences? Does the definition depend on different perspectives (e.g. globalisation from the perspective of consumer, government or the employees)?

Students work in groups. Each group should be asked to produce a poster examining either the advantages or the disadvantages of globalisation for:

- consumers
- local and overseas employees
- firms
- local and overseas governments.

Each group should work on something different (e.g. benefits to consumers, disadvantages to employees).

→

Once the groups have produced their posters, they move around the rooms looking at other posters and adding points where they can. For example, every five minutes they move from one poster to the next. By the end of the process, you should have posters of a number of different aspects of globalisation in which everyone has had some input. These can be displayed on the walls.

For homework, students could be asked to write an essay: 'To what extent is greater globalisation a good thing?'

Teaching Tip

Learning is often most effective when it is fun. 'Top Trumps' is a game that consists of cards that list different facts associated with a particular theme (e.g different cars, sports people or animals). One idea is to ask students to create a set of country cards. They can agree on the list of criteria such as population, income, land size, primary sector as a percentage of the economy and so on. Each student researches one country to produce one card so as a class they end up with a set of country cards with which to play.

To play the game, students choose a particular fact about a country and compare that with the person they are playing against. If one student's data is better than the other person's, the first one wins and gets their card. The aim is to collect all the cards. Possible data source: The World factbook website.

Summary

In this chapter, we have highlighted:

- ways in which teachers and students might develop their global thinking
- the value of different perspectives when solving a problem
- the benefits of global issues in stimulating research and debate.

Reflective practice

13

Dr Paul Beedle, Head of Professional Development
Qualifications, Cambridge International Examinations

'As a teacher you are always learning'

It is easy to say this, isn't it? Is it true? Are you bound to learn just by being a teacher?

You can learn every day from the experience of working with your students, collaborating with your colleagues and playing your part in the life of your school. You can learn also by being receptive to new ideas and approaches, and by applying and evaluating these in practice in your own context.

To be more precise, let us say that as a teacher:

- You **should** always be learning
  to develop your expertise throughout your career for your own fulfilment as a member of the teaching profession and to be as effective as possible in the classroom.
- You **can** always be learning
  if you approach the teaching experience with an open mind, ready to learn and knowing how to reflect on what you are doing in order to improve.

You want your professional development activities to be as relevant as possible to what you do and who you are, and to help change the quality of your teaching and your students' learning – for the better, in terms of outcomes, and for good, in terms of lasting effect. You want to feel that 'it all makes sense' and that you are actively following a path that works for you personally, professionally and career-wise.

So professional learning is about making the most of opportunities and your working environment, bearing in mind who you are, what you are like and how you want to improve. But simply experiencing – thinking about and responding to situations, and absorbing ideas and information – is not necessarily learning. It is through reflection that you can make the most of your experience to deepen and extend your professional skills and understanding.

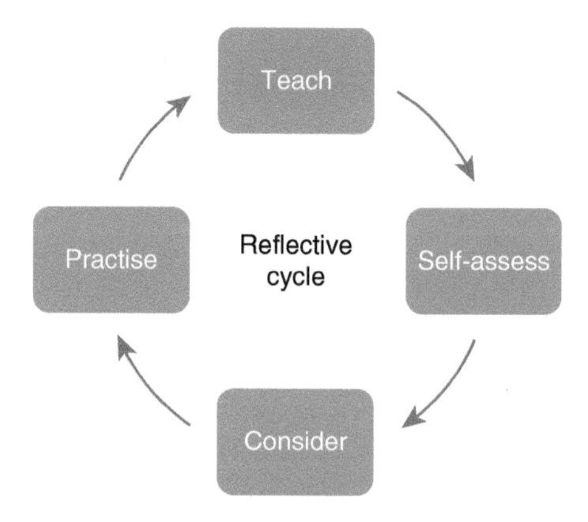

Figure 13.1

In this chapter, we will focus on three *essentials* of reflective practice, explaining in principle and in practice how you can support your own continuing professional development:

1 **Focusing** on what you want to learn about and why.
2 **Challenging** yourself and others to go beyond description and assumptions to critical analysis and evaluation.
3 **Sharing** what you are learning with colleagues – to enrich understanding and enhance the quality of practice.

These essentials will help you as you apply and adapt the rich ideas and approaches in this book in your own particular context. They will also help you if you are, or are about to be, taking part in a Cambridge Professional Development Qualification (Cambridge PDQ) programme, to make the most of your programme, develop your portfolio and gain the qualification.

1 Focus

In principle

Given the multiple dimensions and demands of being a teacher, you might be tempted to try to cover 'everything' in your professional development but you will then not have the time to go beneath the surface much at all. Likewise, attending many different training events will certainly keep you very busy but it is unlikely that these will simply add up to improving your thinking and practice in sustainable and systematic ways.

Teachers who are beginning an organised programme of professional learning find that it is most helpful to select particular ideas, approaches and topics which are relevant to their own situation and their school's priorities. They can then be clear about their professional learning goals, and how their own learning contributes to improving their students' learning outcomes. They deliberately choose activities that help make sense of their practice with their students in their school and have clear overall purpose.

It is one thing achieving focus, and another maintaining this over time. When the going gets tough, because it is difficult either to understand or become familiar with new ideas and practices, or to balance learning time with the demands of work and life, it really helps to have a mission – to know why you want to learn something as well as what that something is. Make sure that this is a purpose which you feel genuinely belongs to you and in which you have a keen interest, rather than it being something given to you or imposed on you. Articulate your focus not just by writing it down but by 'pitching' it to a colleague whose opinion you trust and taking note of their feedback.

In practice

- Plan
  What is my goal and how will I approach the activity?

  Select an approach that is new to you, but make sure that you understand the thinking behind this and that it is relevant to your students' learning. Do it for real effect, not for show.

- Monitor
  Am I making progress towards my goal; do I need to try a different approach?

  Take time during your professional development programme to review how far and well you are developing your understanding of theory and practice. What can you do to get more out of the experience, for example by discussing issues with your mentor, researching particular points, and asking your colleagues for their advice?

- Evaluate
  What went well, what could have been better, what have I learned for next time?

  Evaluation can sometimes be seen as a 'duty to perform' – like clearing up after the event – rather than the pivotal moment in learning that it really is. Evaluate not because you are told you have to; evaluate to make sense of the learning experience you have been through and what it means to you, and to plan ahead to see what you can do in the future.

This cycle of planning, monitoring and evaluation is just as relevant to you as a professional learner as to your students as learners. Be actively in charge of your learning and take appropriate actions. Make your professional development work for you. Of course your professional development programme leaders, trainers and mentors will guide and support you in your learning, but you are at the heart of your own learning experience, not on the receiving end of something that is cast in stone. Those who assist and advise you on your professional development want you and your colleagues to get the best out of the experience, and need your feedback along the way so that if necessary they can adapt and improve what they are devising.

2 Challenge

In principle

Reflection is a constructive process that helps the individual teacher to improve their thinking and practice. It involves regularly asking questions of yourself about your developing ideas and experience, and keeping track of your developing thinking, for example in a reflective journal. Reflection is continuous, rather than a one-off experience. Being honest with yourself means thinking hard, prompting yourself to go beyond your first thoughts about a new experience and to avoid taking for granted your opinions about something to which you are accustomed. Be a critical friend to yourself.

In the Cambridge PDQ Certificate in Teaching and Learning, for example, teachers take a fresh look at the concepts and processes of learning and challenge their own assumptions. They engage with theory and models of effective teaching and learning, and open their minds through observing experienced practitioners, applying new ideas in practice and listening to formative feedback from mentors and colleagues. To evidence in their assessed portfolio how they have learned from this experience, they not only present records of observed practice but also critical analysis showing understanding of how and why practices work and how they can be put into different contexts successfully.

The Cambridge PDQ syllabuses set out key questions to focus professional learning and the portfolio templates prompts to help you. These questions provide a framework for reflection. They are open-ended and will not only stimulate your thinking but lead to lively group discussion. The discipline of asking yourself and others questions such as 'Why?' 'How do we know?' 'What is the evidence?' 'What are the conditions?' leads to thoughtful and intelligent practice.

In practice

Challenge:

- Yourself, as you reflect on an experience, to be more critical in your thinking. For example, rather than simply describing what happened, analyse why it happened and its significance, and what might have happened if conditions had been different.
- Theory – by understanding and analysing the argument, and evaluating the evidence that supports the theory. Don't simply accept a theory as a given fact – be sure that you feel that the ideas make sense and that there is positive value in applying them in practice.
- Convention – the concept of 'best practice(s)' is as good as we know now, on the basis of the body of evidence, for example on the effect size of impact of a particular approach on learning outcomes. By using an approach in an informed way and with a critical eye, you can evaluate the approach relating to your particular situation.

3 Share

In principle

Schools are such busy places, and yet teachers can feel they are working on their own for long periods because of the intensity of their workload as they focus on all that is involved in teaching their students. We know that a crucial part of our students' active learning is the opportunity to collaborate with their peers in order to investigate, create and communicate. Just so with professional learning: teachers learn best through engagement with their peers, in their own school and beyond. Discussion and interaction with colleagues, focused on learning and student outcomes, and carried out in a culture of openness, trust and respect, helps each member of the community of practice in the school clarify and sharpen their understanding and enhance their practice.

This is why the best professional learning programmes incorporate collaborative learning, and pivotal moments are designed into the programme for this to happen frequently over time: formally in guided learning sessions such as workshops and more informally in opportunities such as study group, teach meets and discussion, both face-to-face and online.

In practice

Go beyond expectations!

In the Cambridge PDQ syllabus, each candidate needs to carry out an observation of an experienced practitioner and to be observed formatively themselves by their mentor on a small number of occasions. This is the formal requirement in terms of evidence of practice within the portfolio for the qualification. The expectation is that these are not the only times that teachers will observe and be observed for professional learning purposes (rather than performance appraisal).

However, the more that teachers can observe each other's teaching, the better; sharing of practice leads to advancement of shared knowledge and understanding of aspects of teaching and learning, and development of agreed shared 'best practice'.

So:

- open your classroom door to observation
- share with your closest colleague(s) when you are trying out a fresh approach, for example an idea in this book
- ask them to look for particular aspects in the lesson, especially how students are engaging with the approach – pose an observation question
- reflect with them after the lesson on what you and they have learned from the experience – pose an evaluation question
- go and observe them as they do the same
- after a number of lessons, discuss with your colleagues how you can build on your peer observation with common purpose, for example lesson study
- share with your other colleagues in the school what you are gaining from this collaboration and encourage them to do the same
- always have question(s) to focus observations and focus these question(s) on student outcomes.

Pathways

The short-term effects of professional development are very much centred on teachers' students. For example, the professional learning in a Cambridge PDQ programme should lead directly and quickly to changes in the ways your students learn. All teachers have this at heart – the desire to help their students learn better.

The long-term effects of professional development are more teacher-centric. During their career over, say, 30 years, a teacher may teach many thousand lessons. There are many good reasons for a teacher to keep up-to-date with pedagogy, not least to sustain their enjoyment of what they do.

Each teacher will follow their own career pathway, taking into account many factors. We do work within systems, at school and wider level, involving salary and appointment levels, and professional development can be linked to these as requirement or expectation. However, to a significant extent teachers shape their own career pathway, making decisions along the way. Their pathway is not pre-ordained; there is room for personal choice, opportunity and serendipity. It is for each teacher to judge for themselves how much they wish to venture. A teacher's professional development pathway should reflect and support this.

It is a big decision to embark on an extended programme of professional development, involving a significant commitment of hours of learning and preparation over several months. You need to be as clear as you can be about the immediate and long-term value of such a commitment. Will your programme lead to academic credit as part of a stepped pathway towards Masters level, for example?

Throughout your career, you need to be mindful of the opportunities you have for professional development. Gauge the value of options available at each particular stage in your professional life, both in terms of relevance to your current situation – your students, subject and phase focus, and school – and the future situation(s) of which you are thinking.

14

Understanding the impact of classroom practice on student progress

Lee Davis, Deputy Director for Education,
Cambridge International Examinations

Introduction

Throughout this book, you have been encouraged to adopt a more active approach to teaching and learning and to ensure that formative assessment is embedded into your classroom practice. In addition, you have been asked to develop your students as meta-learners, such that they are able to, as the academic Chris Watkins puts it, 'narrate their own learning' and become more reflective and strategic in how they plan, carry out and then review any given learning activity.

A key question remains, however. How will you know that the new strategies and approaches you intend to adopt have made a significant difference to your students' progress and learning? What, in other words, has been the impact and how will you know?

This chapter looks at how you might go about determining this at the classroom level. It deliberately avoids reference to whole-school student tracking systems, because these are not readily available to all schools and all teachers. Instead, it considers what you can do as an individual teacher to make the learning of your students visible – both to you and anyone else who is interested in how they are doing. It does so by introducing the concept of 'effect sizes' and shows how these can be used by teachers to determine not just whether an intervention works or not but, more importantly, *how well* it works. 'Effect size' is a useful way of quantifying or measuring the size of any difference between two groups or data sets. The aim is to place emphasis on the most important aspect of an intervention or change in teaching approach – the **size of the effect** on student outcomes.

Consider the following scenario:

Over the course of a term, a teacher has worked hard with her students on understanding 'what success looks like' for any given task or activity. She has stressed the importance of everyone being clear about the criteria for success, before students embark upon the chosen task and plan their way through it. She has even got to the point where students have been co-authors of the assessment rubrics used, so that they have been fully engaged in the intended outcomes throughout and can articulate what is required before they have even started. The teacher is happy with developments so far, but has it made a difference to student progress? Has learning increased beyond what we would normally expect for an average student over a term anyway?

Here is an extract from the teacher's markbook.

Student	Sept Task	Nov Task
Katya	13	15
Maria	15	20
Joao	17	23
David	20	18
Mushtaq	23	25
Caio	25	38
Cristina	28	42
Tom	30	35
Hema	32	37
Jennifer	35	40

Figure 14.1

Before we start analysing this data, we must note the following:

- The task given in September was at the start of the term – the task in November was towards the end of the term.
- Both tasks assessed similar skills, knowledge and understanding in the student.
- The maximum mark for each was 50.
- The only variable that has changed over the course of the term is the approaches to teaching and learning by the teacher. All other things are equal.

With that in mind, looking at Figure 14.1, what conclusions might you draw as an external observer?

You might be saying something along the lines of: 'Mushtaq and Katya have made some progress, but not very much. Caio and Cristina appear to have done particularly well. David, on the other hand, appears to be going backwards!'

What can you say about the class as a whole?

Calculating effect sizes

What if we were to apply the concept of 'effect sizes' to the class results in Figure 14.1, so that we could make some more definitive statements about the impact of the interventions over the given time period? Remember, we are doing so in order to understand the size of the effect on student outcomes or progress.

Let's start by understanding how it is calculated.

An effect size is found by calculating 'the standardised mean difference between two data sets or groups'. In essence, this means we are looking for the difference between two averages, while taking into the account the spread of values (in this case, marks) around those averages at the same time.

As a formula, and from Figure 14.1, it looks like the following:

$$\text{Effect size} = \frac{\text{average class mark (after intervention)} - \text{average class mark (before intervention)}}{\text{spread (standard deviation of the class)}}$$

In words: the average mark achieved by the class *before* the teacher introduced her intervention strategies is taken away from the average mark achieved by the class *after* the intervention strategies. This is then divided by the standard deviation[1] of the class as a whole.

[1] The standard deviation is merely a way of expressing by how much the members of a group (in this case, student marks in the class) differ from the average value (or mark) for the group.

Inserting our data into a spreadsheet helps us calculate the effect size as follows:

	A	B	C
1	Student	September Task	November Task
2	Katya	13	15
3	Maria	15	20
4	Joao	17	23
5	David	20	18
6	Mushtaq	23	25
7	Caio	25	38
8	Cristina	28	42
9	Tom	30	35
10	Hema	32	37
11	Jennifer	35	40
12			
13	Average mark	23.8 = AVERAGE (B2:B11)	29.3 = AVERAGE (C2:C11)
14	Standard deviation	7.5 = STDEV (B2:B11)	10.11 = STDEV (C2:C11)

Figure 14.2

Therefore, the effect size for this class $= \dfrac{29.3 - 23.8}{8.8} = 0.62$

But what does this mean?

Interpreting effect sizes for classroom practice

In pure statistical terms, a 0.62 effect size means that the average student mark **after** the intervention by the teacher, is 0.62 standard deviations above the average student mark **before** the intervention.

We can state this in another way: the post-intervention average mark now exceeds 61% of the student marks previously.

Going further, we can also say that the average student mark, post-intervention, would have placed a student in the top four in the class previously. You can see this visually in Figure 14.2 where 29.3 (the class average after the teacher's interventions) would have been between Cristina's and Tom's marks in the September task.

This is good, isn't it? As a teacher, would you be happy with this progress by the class over the term?

To help understand effect sizes further, and therefore how well or otherwise the teacher has done above, let us look at how they are used in large-scale studies as well as research into educational effectiveness more broadly. We will then turn our attention to what really matters – talking about student learning.

Effect sizes in research

We know from results analyses of the Program for International Student Assessment (PISA) and the Trends in International Mathematics and Science Study (TIMMS) that, across the world, a year's schooling leads to an effect size of 0.4. John Hattie and his team at The University of Melbourne reached similar conclusions when looking at over 900 meta-analyses of classroom and whole-school interventions to improve student learning – 240 million students later, the result was an effect size of 0.4 on average for all these strategies.

What this means, then, is that any teacher achieving an effect size of greater than 0.4 is doing better than expected (than the average) over the course of a year. From our example above, not only are the students making better than expected progress, they are also doing so in just one term.

Here is something else to consider. In England, the distribution of GCSE grades in Maths and English have standard deviations of between 1.5 and 1.8 grades (A*, A, B, C, etc.), so an improvement of one GCSE grade represents an effect size of between 0.5 and 0.7. This means that, in the context of secondary schools, introducing a change in classroom practice of 0.62 (as the teacher achieved above) would result in an improvement of about one GCSE grade for each student in the subject.

Furthermore, for a school in which 50% of students were previously attaining five or more A*–C grades, this percentage (assuming the effect size of 0.62 applied equally across all subjects and all other things being equal) the percentage would rise to 73%.

Now, that's something worth knowing.

What next for your classroom practice? Talking about student learning

Given what we now know about effect sizes, what might be the practical next steps for you as a teacher?

Firstly, try calculating effect sizes for yourself, using marks and scores for your students that are comparable, e.g. student performance on key skills in maths, reading, writing, science practicals, etc. Become familiar with how they are calculated so that you can then start interrogating them 'intelligently'.

Do the results indicate progress was made? If so, how much is attributable to the interventions you have introduced?

Try calculating effect sizes for each individual student, in addition to your class, to make their progress visible too. To help illustrate this, let us return to the comments we were making about the progress of some students in Figure 14.1. We thought Cristina and Caio did very well and we had grave concerns about David. Individual effect sizes for the class of students would help us shed light on this further:

Student	September Task	November task	Individual Effect Size
Katya	13	15	0.22*
Maria	15	20	0.55
Joao	17	23	0.66
David	20	18	-0.22
Mushtaq	23	25	0.22
Caio	25	38	1.43
Cristina	28	42	1.54
Tom	30	35	0.55
Hema	32	37	0.55
Jennifer	35	40	0.55

* The individual effect size for each student above is calculated by taking their September mark away from their November mark and then dividing by the standard deviation for the class – in this case 8.8.

Figure 14.3

If these were your students, what questions would you now ask of yourself, of your students and even of your colleagues, to help you understand why the results are as they are and how learning is best achieved? Remember, an effect size of 0.4 is our benchmark, so who is doing better than that? Who is not making the progress we would expect?

David's situation immediately stands out, doesn't it? A negative effect size implies learning has regressed. So, what has happened, and how will we draw alongside him to find out what the issues are and how best to address them?

Why did Caio and Cristina do so well, considering they were just above average previously? Effect sizes of 1.43 and 1.54 respectively are significantly above the benchmark, so what has changed from their perspective? Perhaps they responded particularly positively to developing assessment rubrics together. Perhaps learning had sometimes been a mystery to them before, but with success criteria now made clear, this obstacle to learning had been removed.

We don't know the answers to these questions, but they would be great to ask, wouldn't they? So go ahead and ask them. Engage in dialogue with your students, and see how their own ability to discuss their learning has changed and developed. This will be as powerful a way as any of discovering whether your new approaches to teaching and learning have had an impact and it ultimately puts data, such as effect sizes, into context.

Concluding remarks

Effect sizes are a very effective means of helping you understand the impact of your classroom practice upon student progress. If you change your teaching strategies in some way, calculating effect sizes, for both the class and each individual student, helps you determine not just *if* learning has improved, but by *how much*.

They are, though, only part of the process. As teachers, we must look at the data carefully and intelligently in order to understand 'why'. Why did some students do better than others? Why did some not make any progress at all? Use effect sizes as a starting point, not the end in itself.

Ensure that you don't do this in isolation – collaborate with others and share this approach with them. What are your colleagues finding in their classes, in their subjects? Are the same students making the same progress across the curriculum? If there are differences, what might account for them?

In answering such questions, we will be in a much better position to determine next steps in the learning process for students. After all, isn't that our primary purpose as teachers?

Acknowledgements, further reading and resources

This chapter has drawn extensively on the influential work of the academics John Hattie and Robert Coe. You are encouraged to look at the following resources to develop your understanding further:

Hattie, J. (2012). *Visible Learning for Teachers – Maximising Impact on Learning*. London and New York: Routledge.

Coe, R. (2002). *It's the Effect Size, Stupid. What effect size is and why it is important.* Paper presented at the Annual Conference of The British Educational Research Association, University of Exeter, England, 12–14 September, 2002. A version of the paper is available online on the University of Leeds website.

The Centre for Evaluation and Monitoring, University of Durham, has produced a very useful effect size calculator (available from their website). Note that it also calculates a confidence interval for any effect size generated. Confidence intervals are useful in helping you understand the margin for error of an effect size you are reporting for your class. These are particularly important when the sample size is small, which will inevitably be the case for most classroom teachers.

Recommended reading

15

For a deeper understanding of the Cambridge approach, refer to the Cambridge International Examinations website (www.cie.org.uk/teaching-and-learning) where you will find the following in-depth guides:

Implementing the curriculum with Cambridge; a guide for school leaders.

Developing your school with Cambridge; a guide for school leaders.

Education briefs for a number of topics, such as active learning and bilingual education. Each brief includes information about the challenges and benefits of different approaches to teaching, practical tips, lists of resources.

Getting started with... These are interactive resources to help to explore and develop areas of teaching and learning. They include practical examples, reflective questions, and experiences from teachers and researchers.

For further support around becoming a Cambridge school visit cambridge-community.org.uk.

The resources in this section can be used as a supplement to your learning, to build upon your awareness of Business and Economics teaching and the pedagogical themes in this series.

Online resources

The Economics, Business and Enterprise Association website has news and articles on Business and Economics education.

Teaching ideas for Economics can be found on the Economics Network website. This includes a question bank and an ideas bank. These activities are designed mainly for university students but you will be able to find some resources that are useful and others that inspire.

Ideas on different teaching strategies for innovative economics teaching can be found on the Starting Point: Teaching and Learning Economics website.

Articles

Bergmann, J., & Sams, A. (2012). *Flip your classroom: Reach every student in every class every day*. Eugene, OR: International Society for Technology in Education.

Bergmann, J., Overmyer, J., & Wilie, B. (2013). *The flipped class: What it is and what it is not.*

Brant, J. (2003). "Business and economics education: the development of subject expertise and creativity in beginning teachers of business and economics education." *Edukacja, 81 (1)*, 116–124.

Brant, J.W. (2015). What's wrong with secondary school economics and how teachers can make it right – Methodological critique and pedagogical possibilities. *Journal of Social Science Education, 14 (4)*, 7–16. doi:10.2390/jsse-v14-i4-1391.

Brant, J., & Cullimore, D. (2012). Participation, progression and value added: Business and economics for 14–19 year olds in England. *Curriculum Journal, 23 (1)*, 79–98.

Brant, J. & Davies P. (2006). *Business, Economics and Enterprise: Teaching School Subjects 11–19*, London: Routledge Falmer 256 pp.

Chu, Shiou-Yen (2014). "An assessment of teaching Economics with The Simpsons." *International Journal of Pluralism and Economics Education, 5 (2)*, 180–196.

Collett-Scmitt, K., Guest, R. & Davies, P. (2014). "Assessing student understanding of price and opportunity cost through a hybrid test instrument: an exploratory study," *Journal of Economics and Economics Education, 16 (1)*, 115–134.

Davies, P. (2009). "Improving the quality of students' arguments through 'assessment for learning', " *Journal of Social Science Education, 8*, 94–104.

Davies, P. (2012), "Threshold concepts in economics education", in Hoyt, G.M. and McGoldrick, K. (Eds), *International Handbook on Teaching and Learning in Economics*, Edward Elgar, Cheltenham

Davis, M.E. (2015). "Bringing imagination back to the classroom: a model for creative arts in Economics." *International Review of Economics Education, 19*, 1–12.

Diamond, Arthur M. (2009). "Using video clips to teach creative destruction." *The Journal of Private Enterprise, 25 (1)*, 151–161.

Dunne, D. & Brooks, K. (2004). *Teaching with cases*. Halifax, NS: Society for Teaching and Learning in Higher Education.

Gillis, M.T. & Hall, J.C. (2010). "Using The Simpsons to improve economic instruction through policy analysis." *American Economist, 55 (1)*, 84.

Martin, J. & Abbott, I. (2005). *Teaching Business Education 14–19*. London: David Fulton Publishers.

Lin, Tin-Chun & Dunphy, S.M. (2013). "Using the crossword puzzle exercise in introductory Microeconomics to accelerate student learning". *Journal of Education for Business*, Abingdon Mar/Apr, *88 (2)*, 88–93.

Meyer, J.H.F. (2010), "Helping our students: learning, metalearning, and threshold concepts", in Christensen Hughes, J. and Mighty, J. (Eds), Taking Stock: Research on Teaching and Learning in Higher Education, McGill-Queen's University Press, Montreal and Kingston.

Podemska-Mikluch, M. & Deyo, D. (2014). "It's just like magic: the Economics of Harry Potter." *Journal of Economics and Finance Education, 13 (2)*, 90–98.

Podemska-Mikluch, M. Deyo, D. & Mitchell, D.T. (2015). "Public choice lessons from the wizarding world of Harry Potter." *The Journal of Private Enterprise*, 3*1(1)*, 57–69.

Salemi, M. K. (2002). "An illustrated case for active learning." *Southern Economic Journal, 68 (3)*, 721–731.

Salemi, M. K. (2005). "Teaching Economic literacy: why, what and how." *International Review of Economics Education, 4 (2)*, 46–57.

Van Horn, and Van Horn, M. (2013). "What would Adam Smith have on his iPod? Uses of Music in Teaching the History of Economic Thought." *Journal of Economic Education, 44 (1)*, 64–73.

Books

Brown, Peter, C. & Mark A. McDaniel (2014). *Make It Stick: The Science of Successful Learning*. Cambridge: Belknap Press.

Watkins C (2015) *Meta-Learning in Classrooms*. The SAGE Handbook of Learning. Edited by Scott D. and Hargreaves E. London: Sage Publications Ltd.

Index

Note: The letters 'f' following locators refer to figures.